Children
of a
Greater
GOD

Terry W. Glaspey

HARVEST HOUSE PUBLISHERS
Eugene, Oregon 97402

CHILDREN OF A GREATER GOD

Copyright © 1995 by Harvest House Publishers
Eugene, Oregon 97402

Library of Congress Cataloging-in-Publication Data

Glaspey, Terry.
     Children of a greater God : awakening your child's moral
     imagination / by Terry Glaspey.
          p. cm.
     ISBN 1-56507-264-2
     1. Christian ethics. 2. Youth—Conduct of life. 3. Moral
     education. I. Glaspey, Terry. II. Title.
     BJ1251.G53   1995
     248.8'2—dc20   94-22293
                                                              CIP

95   96   97   98   99   00   01   —   10   9   8   7   6   5   4   3   2   1

To C. S. Lewis,
whose life and works demonstrated
that reason, imagination, and holiness
could form an integrated whole.

Thanks . . .

To Sally, my wife, whose editorial insight made this a better book than it would have been. Her patience, encouragement, intelligence, and love make her not only the woman I love, but also my best friend.

To Emma and Kathryn, my two sweet daughters—your daddy is very proud of you!

To Larry and Pat Glaspey, whose unconditional love and unflinching integrity continue to provide role models for me. One could not ask for better parents.

To Dean and Karen Andreola, good friends and sharers in the vision. Your encouragement to put my ideas to paper played a significant role in making this book a reality.

To my friends at Harvest House, it is a pleasure to work with you. Special thanks to **Steve Miller** and **Bill Jensen** for their valuable suggestions and to **Gloria Chisholm** for adding polish to the final draft of this book. Your work is appreciated.

Contents

Introduction

Part One: The Moral Imagination

1. Being Moral in a Time of Relativism 13
2. Going Beyond the Rules........................ 27
3. What Does Virtue Look Like? 37
4. Making a Habit of Virtue 47

Part Two: The Christian Mind and Spirit

5. Thinking Christianly 57
6. Every Child a Theologian 71
7. In Praise of Tradition 87
8. Spoiling the Egyptians 107
9. The Spiritual Lives of Children 117

Part Three: The Christian Vision

10. The Moral Imagination and Culture 131
11. Television: The One-Eyed Bandit 135
12. The Adventure of Reading Aloud 147
13. The Moral Value of Stories 155
14. The True and the Beautiful 167
15. Music to Calm the Savage Breast 189
16. Taking Fun Seriously 207
17. The Road to Christian Adulthood 215

Appendix: Great Reading for the Family 221

Notes 235

Introduction

Being a parent is a job that requires a great deal of skill. There are no classes you can take or books you can read to guarantee that you will master the task of parenting. Instead, you are thrown back on your own limitations or the sometimes dubious example of your own parents. Untrained, you are thrust into a role which is often thankless, always worrisome, and sometimes downright frightening. The rewards are mostly intangible: You receive no payments, no awards or plaques. Instead, the reward of parenting is the pleasure of raising children who grow into mature adults—adults who love God with their whole heart, soul, and mind. Unfortunately (maybe fortunately!), character and maturity are not genetically inherited. Neither does character develop automatically in our children as a result of our priorities and rules being strictly enforced. We all know stories of parents whose kids, once obedient to every command, simply went "off the rails" and messed up their lives. This despite strict rules and firm, loving guidance.

Many commendable books have been written about the necessity of "tough love" in dealing with our children. These books emphasize the necessity of fair but firm discipline in raising our kids. I concur with the biblical injunction that to spare the rod is to spoil the child. And while this author heartily believes in strong parental guidance administered with love, I feel that there is another aspect involved in guiding your child toward moral responsibility. In this book I want to suggest that rules alone do not make a child moral and that unquestioned obedience to a parent is not in itself the goal. We must require more of ourselves. We must instill within our children a vision for the good and moral life. We must create in their heart and mind a clear understanding of the beauty and importance of moral living. And we must help them develop an intellectual framework which will enable them to apply the Christian message to every area of their lives and provide them with the ennobling ability to recognize and appreciate the beauty of truth as it can be seen in literature, the arts, and in the natural world around them.

In this book I hope to provide you with tools and suggestions which will help you raise a child who is able to cope with the intense intellectual, cultural, and spiritual challenges which will inevitably surface in these confusing and chaotic times in which we live. It is my hope that this book will help you to construct a strong and vigorous faith in your child's life—one rooted in a moral and spiritual vision of the truly good.

An old-fashioned phrase aptly describes the goal of this book: training the sensibilities. By this I mean the training of your child's thoughts and feelings. By introducing your child to what is truly good, whether it comes in the form of moral character or great art and music, you further the process of training him to be a person whose heart will deeply resonate with the good. This means that the good will have enough of an overwhelming appeal that "when push comes to shove" in the temptations of life, your child will make the right decisions. Educating the sensibilities means training heart, mind, soul, and spirit. It is to train the passions so that we feel passionate about the right things.

As parents we must ask ourselves the question, "What kind of kids do we want to raise?" Are we satisfied with carbon copies of ourselves? Is unquestioning obedience to our rules and commands our goal? Or do we have a vision for moral, spiritual, and intellectual achievements from our kids? It is crucial in any undertaking to have some idea of what you want to achieve, what you imagine your goal or hoped-for end result will be.

I think that we can all agree that our goal is a morally, spiritually, and intellectually mature child—the kind of child who is able to stand up for good in this increasingly difficult time in which we live. A child marked by a growing faith, an intellectual acuity, an aesthetic sensitivity, a discerning spirit, and strong moral character. This is the kind of child which this book endeavors to help you raise.

This is obviously a lofty goal, but one worth pursuing. There are no magic formulas for building these kinds of characteristics in our children's lives. But in this book we will look at some time-tested ways to introduce our children to what is truly valuable and worthwhile in life. Your challenge is to awaken a moral imagination in your child.

One thing about this book that might surprise you is the number of quotes from classic thinkers like Plato, Augustine, C. S. Lewis, and others. There is a simple reason for this. We can glean much wisdom from the great thinkers of the past. Teaching our children to live and think as virtuous people, as people who demonstrate the character of Christ in their lives, words, and deeds, is not a matter of learning the latest techniques of the child psychologists. It is not a new pursuit, but an age-old one. I invite you to join with me in this pursuit.

PART ONE

The Moral Imagination

The fact that, compared to the inhabitants of Africa and Russia, we still live well, cannot ease the pain of feeling we no longer live nobly.

—John Updike

• • •

1

Being Moral in a Time of Relativism

The Morality of Rules and the Morality of Vision

*W*atching the news on television has become a painful undertaking. A couple of nights ago I flipped on the 11 o'clock news to catch up on the headlines before I went to bed. But what I heard in a few short minutes made sleeping difficult. One story was about a five-year-old killed in the cross fire of gang warfare not far from where I live. She died in her mother's arms. A report on a string of burglaries included a murder. The anchorman warned against a growing trend—car-jackings in which the perpetrators dragged motorists out of their cars at intersections. If you tried to resist, you would likely be run over. Finally, I listened to a report on high schools nearby which had, of necessity, equipped a number of new classrooms for the growing number of students who had children of their own. Many of these youngsters could not find childcare for their newborns, so the school was testing a new program that made it possible for the babies to be in school with their mothers.

A Culture in Moral Chaos

It's not easy being a kid nowadays. Of course it was never easy being a kid, never easy to navigate one's way through the moral pitfalls that lay in wait for you. But as my generation was growing up, about the worst thing that could happen in school was getting beat up by the school bully. Today, in many schools, you could end up dead from a knife or a gunshot wound.

At one time you could pretty much count on you and your peers at least agreeing on what was morally wrong, even if few found the moral strength to resist temptation. Today, many question whether there is a right and a wrong in the first place.

It is a fundamental and undeniable reality that our culture is in moral crisis. Many who are now parents grew up, like me, in the permissive era of the sixties—a time that celebrated the overthrow of all moral authority and reveled in smashing all the norms of society. The sixties *era* was largely about celebrating the potential for breaking free from conformity and rules. The sixties *error* was the belief that people would reach their "human potential" by casting aside all restraints and indulging their passions and desires. "If it feels good, do it," was the operative phrase for the sixties generation. While appreciating the need to break free from mere conformity and to find adequate and honest self-expression, the permissiveness of the sixties has borne bitter fruit in the lawlessness and moral chaos of our own times. We have come to understand that human beings must have standards by which to live their lives or we will all lapse together into a modern and technologically advanced form of barbarism.

The Age of Moral Relativism

One would think that we could point to where we have

transgressed God's moral laws and begin by reaffirming these moral directives as a pattern for starting over. Unfortunately, this is no longer the case, for we live in a time of moral relativism. Few in our society believe that there is anything at all that can be clearly labeled right or wrong. It is, they say, "relative"—all a matter of one's own personal perspective. Everyone, we are told, must construct his own "value system." What is right for one may not be right for another. Each action must be judged by the circumstances which surround it. We cannot proclaim anything right or wrong. Ethical standards arise from what is culturally normative and acceptable, and this may change with each generation. There are, we are told, no absolutes. The biggest sin we can commit is to try to persuade other people that their values are wrong or inadequate. The only absolute is that there are no absolutes!

Our culture believes in morality by majority vote. Imagine if Moses had handled issues of morality the way that our culture does. Can you see him standing before God, clipboard in hand, with the results of his survey of the Israelites: "Ninety percent approve the one about killing, and 78 percent the one about stealing, but you'll never get the one about adultery passed—only a 15-percent approval rate." Our culture seems to feel that the Ten Commandments would be better labeled the "Ten Suggestions."

What can we do to protect our children from falling into the sinful traps which society has set for them? Unfortunately, the ethical system which our culture touts is so often lacking in the moral sense that obedience to God engenders. Sometimes the resulting confusion of priorities would be humorous if the souls of our children were not at stake. Ron Julian, an acquaintance of mine, says it well: "Children are getting the picture that if a woman sleeps around, gets pregnant, has an abortion, and then becomes a lesbian, she has made a personal lifestyle choice, but if she drinks from a styrofoam cup, she has done something morally wrong."[1]

Recently, a high school class was asked, "What should you do in the following situation? You find a purse with $1,000 in it. Should you return it to its owner?" A majority of the students felt that to do so would be foolish and stupid. And yet, I'm willing to bet that when their own personal well-being is at issue, suddenly their values change. These same students, if asked whether their teacher should be allowed to assign grades based on personal feelings toward each individual student, would most likely raise their voices in moral outrage.

Ignoring the implications of an absolute moral system (i.e., that a personal God is at its foundation), the schools are awash in a moral relativism which fails to give children the tools to build a moral system. And the messages in the popular media are of little help in this undertaking. Take for an example this quote from a magazine for teenagers called *Today's Teen*: "Too strict a conscience may make you feel different and unpopular. None of these feelings belong to a healthy personality."

Our schools are not totally ignorant of the problems which our shattered moral system leaves in its wake. Educators have come up with what they feel is the solution to the moral crisis at hand—something called "values clarification." Values clarification is the process of assisting children in developing their own set of moral standards by the use of decision-making games and discussions. In other words, we do not teach them moral standards, but we help them clarify their own moral feelings. For example, in one of the games you are on a ship which is sinking. Only one life raft is available and it can carry only three passengers. On the ship are a priest, a newborn baby with its mother, a mentally retarded boy, the captain, the first mate, a beautiful Hollywood film star, a scientist who is working on a cure for cancer, and yourself. You alone are called on to decide who should be given the opportunity to float to safety in the raft. Pick three. Whom do you save and why? A situation of this sort is called a moral quandary, and the problem is certainly a vexing one. But is this an effective way to teach morals? Two factors make this method of moral inquiry suspect.

First, this is an unreal situation—one that at most only a handful of people in history have ever had to face. Certainly it is highly unlikely that your children will ever have to make such a decision. This method suggests to children that acting morally is simply a matter of examining the issue from every possible angle and determining what is most logical and practical given the set of circumstances. It reduces morality to an intellectual problem, ignoring the fact that the real moral struggles which we face on a daily basis are more a problem of the will than of the mind. We usually know what we should do in a given situation. The problem usually comes in having the moral strength to do what is right. So often, what we want to do is not the same as what we know we should do. "I have the desire to do what is good, but I cannot carry it out. For what I do is not the good I want to do; no, the evil I do not want to do—this I keep on doing" (Romans 7:18,19).

Second, this approach to teaching morals makes a fundamental assumption that I believe is patently false. It assumes that a young person, who has had little life experience and little exposure to the great moral and religious teachings of the Bible and of our culture, could make informed moral choices without reference to the traditional teachings which inform our moral systems. We cannot reinvent the wheel with each succeeding generation. Neither can each generation reinvent the morals by which they live, cavalierly ignoring the teachings of their predecessors. Before we reject what those before us have taught, what they have learned and experienced through the generations, we had better be certain that we have somehow seen more deeply into human nature and the character of God than they ever did. It seems clear to me that only a precious few adolescents are capable of making truly wise decisions on their sexual morals without the input of their parents and wise ethical teachers. A group of preteens, left to themselves, would surely draw many questionable, if not completely off-base, moral conclusions. The instincts and hormones of fallen humanity dwell in force in these young ones.

Also, it must be said that "values clarification" often functions more like a subtle form of propagandizing than anything else. The values of the teachers, rather than those of parents or the children themselves, seem to be most dominant in the group setting. It is a rare teacher who cares so little about his or her own opinions that they are not interposed powerfully into the discussions. Overall, the idea that even the most obviously pernicious opinions must be given free rein of expression and tolerant respect goes a long way toward instilling an attitude of moral relativism in our children. If you are counting on the schools to teach your children to be responsible adults, you might want to give more attention to what the schools are teaching.

Many well-meaning Christian parents think they have the solution to this problem. They feel the answer is to become increasingly strict with their children. If they set down strict and comprehensive rules, so the thought goes, their kids will learn the boundaries and respond accordingly. They believe that if they set a hedge of rules around them, they can protect them and keep them from moral error.

The problem with this solution is that rules are not enough. Rules may help in the short term to protect us from the consequences of vice, but they do not make us virtuous people. If we want our kids to be truly virtuous, we must bequeath to them something more than a set of rules.

Two Kinds of Morality

There are two different kinds of morality: a morality based upon rules and a morality based upon vision. The morality of rules is a morality of specific guidance for specific situations. It is a morality which is clearly marked out and differentiated. It is the morality of the stop sign; it tells us when to stop before we have gone too far. This is useful for many situations but is ultimately inadequate. The kind of morality that can fashion our children into people who are truly virtuous is the morality of vision. This morality comes from a way of seeing life, from a vision for what is truly good.

As children, we are encouraged to follow the rules. If we obey them with some semblance of success, we are deemed "good." If we make a regular practice of breaking or subverting the rules, we are pronounced "bad." It is easy for us to consider ourselves good because we have followed the rules, when inside we are not really good at all. We can meet every expectation of the rules and still be proud, selfish, self-serving, deceitful, and impure. In the Sermon on the Mount, Jesus tells us that mere outward obedience to the laws of God (or the rules) is not enough. We need to be changed and purified on the inside. We must become people of character.

The Morality of Rules

As we grow up, our lives are encircled by rules. Every room in our home is filled with specific prescriptions about how we are to act:

- Don't bounce up and down on the bed.
- Don't throw your dirty clothes on the floor; put them in the hamper.
- Don't run on the stairs.
- Don't flick the light switch on and off.
- Don't stick anything into the electrical sockets.
- Don't leave the refrigerator door open so long while you decide on a snack.
- Don't leave the toilet seat up.

This sense of living in the midst of a cluster of rules does not end when we become adults. Everywhere we turn, we find rules, explicit or implicit, which command our attention. Signs are posted on our streets and highways to tell us how fast we can drive and lines on the roadway clearly mark out the space in which we can drive our vehicle. We cannot simply use any lane we choose and go as fast as we want to. Can you imagine the chaos that would result if our driving were not regulated? Anyone who has driven in New York City probably has some idea.

Rules give us a sense of security and inform us of our limits. And life does enforce limits upon us. Life is complicated at times, and rules help strip it of some of its complications. They provide boundaries. They help us know how to act in specific circumstances. Often, in our homes as well as in society, rules protect us from one another. Rules can keep us from infringing in thoughtless ways on the safety and comfort of other people.

The Morality of Vision

The morality of rules has certain limitations. For one thing, rules are fundamentally negative in their prescription. They tell us what not to do, how not to act. As we have indicated, this can be important in learning to live righteously. However, rules are not successful at giving us a picture of how we should act, what kind of people we should be. The moral rules are the road map; they show us which roads to travel. But a road map is not the same thing as arriving at the destination. What would we think of someone who had traced the route with their finger and then proclaimed to have taken the journey? It is the same way with moral rules. They exist not as ends in themselves, but as markers on the road to becoming a virtuous person.

Romans 2:15 teaches us that we are born with an innate knowledge of the difference between good and evil. "The requirements of the law are written on their hearts, their consciences also bearing witness." But both our sin nature and the corruption of the fallen world in which we live chip away at this moral knowledge, questioning it, justifying the multitude of ways in which we try to evade it.

This is why the morality of vision is so important. It takes us beyond the dos and don'ts. It causes us to see ourselves and the world around us from God's perspective. It is a focus on the good which makes clear to us what falls short of true goodness.

The morality of vision takes us beyond conformity. Sometimes we can grit our teeth and "do the right thing," even though it doesn't make sense to us. But this is difficult and usually ineffective. The morality of vision helps us understand more clearly what is truly good and righteous and makes proper action that much easier. In this book, we have called this "the moral imagination." It is using our God-given abilities to think creatively, putting them into practice in the moral sphere.

Moral imagination is the ability to think clearly and creatively in the realm of moral values, especially when faced with a situation where rules do not suffice. In our increasingly complex world, we and our children will find ourselves up against situations where there is simply no learned rule to apply. I have seen many instances of basically well-raised kids who, on entering college, find themselves in all kinds of unfamiliar situations where they must make moral decisions. When they rack their brains and rehearse Mom and Dad's list of rules, they don't find one that applies. If they haven't learned to think for themselves in the moral realm, drawing on the resources of a well-trained moral imagination, they may not be able to weather the storm. I have, sadly, seen many such young people blown off course. The moral imagination is not a panacea, but it is a valuable heritage we can give to our children. Matthew Arnold wrote, "The world is forwarded by having its attention fixed on the best things." This is what the moral imagination is all about—a richer, fuller, truer vision of reality.

Imagination: Moral and Immoral

The imagination is a powerful force. It is neutral and can be used for good or evil. This is clearly recognized in the Scriptures. "And God saw that the wickedness of man was great in the earth, and that every imagination of the thoughts of his heart was only evil continually" (Genesis 6:5 KJV). The judgment of the flood came about because of moral corruption which was bred in evil imagination.

In Hebrew, the word for *imagination* is *yeser*, which means "to form or create." It is the verb for the act of creativity and is the same verb used for God's actions in creating the earth in the first chapters of Genesis. The question is, Are we creating positive or negative things in our minds?

In the fifth chapter of Matthew, Jesus teaches that the imagining of evil is akin to doing evil. It sets our hearts toward evil and away from God. Lusting after a woman, therefore, is akin to committing adultery with her (Matthew 5:28).

Isaiah 26:3 says, "You will keep in perfect peace him whose mind is steadfast, because he trusts in you." The same verb, *yeser*, is used in this passage for the word translated as "mind." This is the kind of imagination we want to develop. What does it mean to be steadfast? In his book on the biblical perspective of imagination, Old Testament scholar Ronald Allen suggests this is "imagination that is under discipline."[2] This is what the moral imagination is all about—imagination under discipline.

The immoral imagination gives free rein to every corrupt thought that would enter. It exercises its power to imagine new forms of debauchery and wickedness. It is like a boulder careening down a steep slope. Once the immoral imagination is awakened, it often leads to sins of thought or deed. Imagination of this kind can be an escape from reality, a feeding on unreality, a focus on lies at the expense of the truth.

The moral imagination is an imagination under discipline— the discipline of faith. It allows the grace of God to cover its failings but always strives to be under the direction of God. This kind of imagination is a powerful spiritual tool. It helps us to see what others do not, and to see more deeply into people and situations, beyond that which the senses can perceive. It helps us see what God would have us see—the often dimly glimpsed spiritual perspective on people and situations. In a world where we often get so caught up in the here-and-now, imagination gives us the ability to escape from the mundane and the ordinary and enables us to be filled with the wonder of life.

There is a contest going on in our society, and the prize is the hearts and minds of people. Often these hearts and minds cannot be reached through a presentation of biblical dogmas, but will respond more readily to a positive and awe-inspiring vision of reality. Sometimes the first steps of change occur when we present a richer vision of reality. Secularism is so distressingly dull and hopeless. True biblical Christianity is exciting, affirming, and realistic about the human condition. In general, the Christian vision which most believers project today fails to effectively engage the imagination of our culture. This is because we have not often used our God-given gift of creative imagination in presenting and living that vision. But we can change. Let us commit ourselves to giving our children the rich heritage of Christian vision.

Awakening the Moral Imagination

What does it take to cultivate the moral imagination of our children, to awaken within them a vision for what is truly good and noble? The answer to this question will make up the bulk of this book.

First, we must help our children to develop good habits, to foster the kind of self-discipline which will enable them to respond to morally vexing situations in a way that honors God and demonstrates true virtue. When they form good habits, children are empowered to develop "right desiring" and the will and discipline to do as they ought.

Second, we must expose our children to positive role models. Our words and actions must demonstrate (at least in an approximation) what moral goodness looks like. Our own lives are far from our only resource. We can point children to historical figures who manifest godly values and character as well as read them stories which demonstrate virtue in action.

Third, we must help our children develop a Christian intelligence that they might learn to "think Christianly" in the various experiences of life. Too often we work to develop hearts in our children that are soft toward God but fail them in leaving their minds soft as well. If our children are to think Christianly, we must give them a basic theological understanding of the faith, help them understand the riches of the Christian heritage throughout history, and teach them how to discerningly make use of the best that our secular culture offers without buckling under the pressures of the modern world.

Fourth, we must build in our homes an environment conducive to developing a creative, honest, and beautiful character. This means using discernment when it comes to television, radio, and other distractive leisure pursuits. The old saying "garbage in, garbage out" is applicable to more than computer programming.

Fifth, we must expose our children to the beauty both of the created order (nature) and of the artifacts of human creativity (the arts). They should learn to appreciate nature, to see the wondrous hand of God at work around them. They should also learn to appreciate the truly noble and praiseworthy in the visual arts, in music, and in great literature. They should learn to recognize the difference between the shoddy, clichéd popular art which surrounds them and that which is worthy of their contemplation and attention.

The ultimate goal of the moral imagination is not, of course, to make us feel like we have succeeded as parents, or to raise children who will think and feel about everything exactly as we do. God forbid! Our goal is the conversion of our children into "children of a greater God," able to overcome the hereditary and environmental shortcomings of the way we have raised them, able to hold to what is good in their heritage and to be evermore transformed into the character of Christ. What we want is children whose faith and vision will exceed our own—children who, as adults, can be a living message of virtue, intellectual integrity, and loving hope to a needy world.

Virtue is the health and beauty and well-being of the soul, and vice the disease and weakness and deformity of the same.

—Plato

•   •   •

2

Going
Beyond the Rules

Moral Virtue and Moral Vision

$\mathcal{A}$ common theme of modern songs, stories, and movies is the goodness and innocence of the little child. In the movie *E.T.*, for example, we see the young boy who rises above the greed and stupidity of the adults who surround him, to protect the friendly space alien. *Free Willy*, the tale of a boy who releases a captive whale, is another example of this genre. Such stories are based on the notion that children are basically good and uncorrupted, that it is the struggles of growing up, not their inner nature, which causes them to behave badly. Although entertaining and heartwarming, these stories do us a grave disservice if they subtly deceive us about the true nature of the child.

One of the false notions on which modern moral thinking is based is that children are inherently good. The idea is widespread that children in their natural state are more pure, more noble, and more good-natured than adults, and that they exude a sense of innocence which is lost as they grow older and more cynical. This is, at best, a half-truth. In his book *Psychological Seduction*, William Kilpatrick suggests a thought experiment. Imagine, he says, that you found yourself trapped in a land of giants. Would you rather they were adult giants or four-year-old giants? Do you really think you would fare better at the hands of a four-year-old? If so, consider the plight of the family cat and how well he fares around the little ones! A moment's reflection brings us the realization that our chances of being treated humanely are greater with adults. William Golding's powerful novel *The Lord of the Flies* turns on the premise of the fallen nature of all people, including children. In the book, a group of young English schoolboys are shipwrecked on an island with no adults present, and left to fend for themselves. In short order they degenerate into the most brutal and barbaric behavior, fighting and killing to establish power and territory. It is a frightening and sobering vision, but a much-needed corrective to the false romanticization of children. Romans 3:23 does not mince words: "All have sinned and fall short of the glory of God."

Children have the same sin nature that adults do, and a greater susceptibility to be ruled by it. A couple of hours spent observing the play of children reveals that they are marked by self-centeredness, the struggle for power, self-will, and childish whims. Kids regularly snatch toys from one another, fight and hit each other, refuse to share, and lie outrageously to cover their wrongdoings. The problem with children is the same as it is with adults. They have a fallen nature which needs to be corrected and redirected. Children are gardens which must be tended. They cannot be left to themselves or to the state of nature. They will be choked by the weeds of selfishness and the thistles of vice. Former president Ronald Reagan once said, "We don't expect children to discover the principles of calculus on their own, but some would give them no guidance when it comes to ethics, morality and values."

Our society has, for the most part, lost sight of the imperative of moral education. We are concerned that our children learn the educational necessities, but we give little thought or effort to their moral education. We fill their brains with information but too often fail to fill their hearts with virtue.

Virtue is a word that has largely fallen out of use in our modern world. We might label someone as "good" or "kind," but rarely would the word *virtuous* come to mind in describing another person. If we as parents and teachers wish to equip our children to deal with the temptations of the modern world, we must teach them to be people of virtue, people whose inner being is so infused with good that their outward actions manifest purity and integrity of thought and feeling. So what then is virtue? Let us examine first what it is not, then we will attempt to define it by examining its characteristics.

False Conceptions of Virtue

Virtue is not the same thing as knowledge. Knowing a moral code does not make one virtuous. Memorizing a set of rules or principles may be useful, but doing so doesn't mean we will be virtuous people. An intellectual knowledge of what is right or wrong is not the same thing as doing right or wrong. To know good is not necessarily to do good. We may know all about the philosophy of ethics and not be an ethical person. William Bennett gives an example from his teaching experience:

> While I was teaching at the University of Wisconsin in the mid-seventies I saw the members of a seminar on advanced ethics, led by the professor, raid a broken soft-drink machine during a break and steal twenty cans of soda. I told them that what they were doing was wrong and that the deliveryman might be forced to pay for the shortfall out of his own pocket. The professor of advanced ethics was unmoved; he reconvened the seminar for further elaborations of ethical dilemmas. Talking a

> good game is not the same as playing one; or if one prefers the more familiar proverb, actions speak louder than words.[1]

It is one thing to espouse virtue; it is quite another thing to live virtuously. The ability to define a character quality is not the same thing as possessing it. Believing passionately in an ideal is not the same thing as acting upon it. I knew a man who espoused the idea that all people are created in God's image and are therefore worthy of respect. He gave the lie to his own teaching by being rude to waiters and waitresses and demonstrating unrealistic expectations for service. In this area of his life he showed a lack of character, even though he knew the right things to say and believed the right things in his head. But virtue is a matter of the heart and will, more than it is a matter of the mind.

Virtue is not simply obedience to a set of rules. This is the mistake we make when we depend upon the morality of rules. Right actions done for the wrong reason do not produce the inner qualities of character which we call virtue. As C. S. Lewis wrote, "We might think that God wanted simply obedience to a set of rules: whereas, He really wants people of a particular sort."[2]

Virtue is not old-fashioned or repressive. We sometimes present virtue as so "straight-laced" that we give the impression it is a negative attainment. Instead of seeing it as a passionate, positive desire for good (and power over the unrelenting cravings of our lower nature), we tend to see it as simply the absence of vices. But virtue is a positive moral force. G. K. Chesterton writes, "Virtue is not the absence of vices or the avoidance of moral dangers; virtue is a vivid and separate thing."[3] This vision of virtue as a positive is something that we can encourage our children to get enthusiastic about. It is something exciting, heroic, and courageous. One reason the writings of C. S. Lewis, George MacDonald, and J. R. R. Tolkien are so powerful is that these authors know how to show the power and fascination of goodness. Whereas in many books the evil characters are really the most interesting and hold the deepest fascination, the group of writers above (often referred to as the "Inklings") present the true nature of evil as petty, self-absorbed, and banal. They show us that it is good which is truly the most fascinating because it challenges us to rise above our sinful instincts and desires to become better people. This, ultimately, is what virtue is all about.

Defining Virtue

Our lives are a battleground for good and evil. Every day, every decision moves us in the direction of righteousness or in the direction of depravity. Morality is not an abstract question or a cluster of issues which we face infrequently—it is the warp and weave of our lives. Henry David Thoreau captured this well in his statement, "Our whole life is startlingly moral. There is never an instant's truce between virtue and vice." This being the case, Thoreau quite accurately concludes that "goodness is the only investment that never fails."

And goodness is an investment which does not come easily and automatically. Effort and energy must be expended on the project of becoming virtuous people. Virtue comes by training ourselves to desire the good, to seek what is upright and holy. The term *training* offers us an accurate picture of what is involved. Becoming a virtuous person requires the marshaling of all our human resources to strive after goodness. Just as an athlete pursues rigorous training to prepare the physical body, so we must rigorously train ourselves into right living. It is not often easy to refuse debauched pleasures and to ignore the temptations which lie before us. The enemy of our soul seeks ways that he may devour us, and we must flee from the false luster of sinful action. A moral struggle with temptation is more like a physical battle than a mental problem. This is why Paul uses the image of warfare in exposing the spiritual struggle which we face with the enemy (Ephesians 6).

"Nature does not give a man virtue," wrote the Roman philosopher Seneca. "The process of becoming a good man is an art."[4]

Left to our natural instincts we would not be virtuous people. Because of our fallen nature, vice is our natural response. If we would be virtuous people, we need someone to show us the way. "Vice quickly creeps in; virtue is difficult to find; she requires ruler and guide. But vice can be acquired even without a tutor."[5] Since we all learn best by imitation, as parents and teachers we must present to our children virtuous role models. Virtue cannot be accurately defined in abstract terms. To be truly understood we must see it in action. If we espouse the importance of good character but do not show it in our actions and decisions, we present a rather pale demonstration of the power and beauty of virtue. Although we will doubtless fail miserably from time to time, our genuine demonstration of the ability to overcome temptation and the lure of convenience will demonstrate to our kids that there is a better way of living than simply being controlled by our emotions and the whims of pleasure-seeking. Even willingness to admit our failures and to strive to correct our faults delivers a powerful message. Examples of moral heroism are so important for our children to see.

In addition to our own example, we must at every opportunity point our children to those who are models of virtue. If we fail to do this, our children will choose their own role models—often amoral rock singers, self-absorbed actors, and arrogant athletes. Introduce your children to historical examples of people who stood firmly for the principles they believed in. Help them see that virtue sometimes extracts a price, but that it is always a price worth paying.

If we look to the past, we find many heroes and heroines who can serve as models for principled decisionmaking and moral courage: Daniel, Socrates, Jesus Christ, the Christian martyrs, Thomas More, John Wycliffe, Catherine Booth, Corrie Ten Boom, Martin Luther King. Spend time with your children reading and discussing the biographies of these heroic figures. In addition to historical examples, literature presents us with many examples: the title character of the book *Jane Eyre*, Alyosha from Dostoevski's *The Brothers Karamazov*,

Frodo and Sam Gamgee from *The Lord of the Rings*, Sidney Carnot from *A Tale of Two Cities*, and several of the characters from Solzhenitsyn's *The First Circle*. Even more common in literature are the stories of those who pay the price for their lack of moral character: Tolstoy's *Anna Karenina*, Lawrence Wentworth from Charles Williams's haunting *The Descent into Hell*, and Goethe's *Faust*.

We are ready, then, to define virtue. Virtue is the ability and power to chase good, which arises from a transformation of our heart and mind. If we are not virtuous people, we are controlled by the desires and tendencies of our fallen nature.

In our society we talk a lot about freedom. By this we usually mean the freedom to do what we want to do. But virtue is a higher freedom—the freedom to not do what we know we should not do. It is the freedom to resist the control of our lusts and volatile emotions and to make holy, just, and righteous decisions. True freedom is the ability to obey God's commands and to act as we know we ought. We might call this wisdom, which is the insight that sees into the ultimate issues that lie beneath our desires and wishes. We are wise when we can see our proper place in God's plan and act accordingly. This has always been the pursuit of the truly wise—a pursuit that today seems less sought after. In *The Abolition of Man*, C. S. Lewis draws an important distinction between our own time and the ancient search for wisdom:

> For the wise men of old, the cardinal problem of human life was how to conform the soul to objective reality, and the solution was wisdom, self-discipline, and virtue. For the modern, the cardinal problem is how to conform reality to the wishes of man, and the solution is technique.[6]

Where the ancients sought after truth, too often we are more concerned with finding ways to make our lives easier or more pleasurable. We search for earthly treasures; they sought for eternal ones. We seek ways to make our lives easier; they sought ways to make themselves better.

All of us want pleasure and happiness. Nobody desires to be unhappy. But much depends on what we value as real pleasure. A natural prerequisite for virtue is to learn to desire the right things, to take joy in the pleasures of the good, to find delight in the things of God, to feel the satisfaction that comes from serving God and from being a person of character. Thomas Aquinas said it well: "No man can live without delight, and that is why a man deprived of spiritual joy goes over to carnal pleasures." If we find our joy in that which is truly good, we will not waste our lives chasing after transient pleasures.

This brings us to a final and important truth. As we seek to be virtuous, we must understand that we can only achieve it in relationship with God. Truly, we can reach a level of human goodness by willpower and intestinal fortitude, but it is only a shadowy image of the true virtue which comes from our participation in the character of Christ. Jesus was our model of true virtue, real integrity, powerful vision, and uncompromising character. True virtue is related to true spirituality. As Augustine writes, "No one without true piety—that is, true worship of the true God—can have true virtue."[7] True worship changes us; it puts our lives in perspective and it humbles our pride. To worship God and to feel His presence in our lives changes our orientation so that virtue flows from a changed heart. It is only in God that we can obtain a true vision of virtue because He is the one who reveals the truth.

As parents, it is up to us to help our children capture a picture of goodness, and to instill in them a vision of virtue that is rich and meaningful and truly pleasurable because it is fixed upon the right things. When we gain a true glimpse of the good, the question becomes, Why would we ever want to be bad? Samuel Johnson wrote, "Virtue presented singly to the imagination or the reason is so well recommended by its own graces and so strongly presented by arguments, that a good man wonders how any can be bad."

Of course, because of our fallen nature, we will always struggle with the temptation to overlook the good and do the expedient or pleasurable. But the vision of virtue provides new insight into the battle we face, throws a new light on our earthly existence, and provides a powerful weapon for gaining victory in this battle. The life of faith does not denigrate earthly life or make it seem inconsequential. On the contrary, it enriches and ennobles life. It gives us a passion for goodness that is a marvelous alternative to the moral drift of our culture. To live for the good is to live life to its fullest. To live for the good is to live with joy.

. . . a man who perseveres in just actions gets in the end a certain quality of character. Now it is that quality rather than the particular actions which we mean when we talk of 'virtue.'

—C. S. Lewis

• • •

3

What Does Virtue Look Like?

Road Maps to Moral Living

*G*eorge's stubbornness was reflective of a trait many men share: He hated to ask for directions. George and Margaret were trying to make it on time to the wedding of a dear friend which was being held downtown in a big city which they had visited only twice before. George was certain he had driven by the First Baptist Church in the past, and he was sure he could find his way there again with little difficulty. Margaret grew increasingly restless as the moments ticked past and George had still not located the church. She knew, of course, that George would never agree to stop at a service station and ask for directions. Somehow, in twisted male logic, to do so was to admit defeat. Real men do not stop to ask for directions. So Margaret suggested they pull off to the side of the road and consult the map she was sure was buried somewhere in the glove compartment. He muttered that they would find the church soon; to stop would be to waste valuable time.

They eventually did find the church, realizing they had passed within a block of it 20 minutes earlier. They arrived just in time to see the wedding car pull away from the curb, trailing its cans and streamers. If real men don't ask for directions, real men arrive real late.

Maps exist to help us traverse the path to moral character. These maps, the virtues, help us see where we need to go and who we need to be, if we are to manifest moral character in our lives. In contemplating how to teach our children to be virtuous, we must have some sort of vision in our minds of what virtue looks like. We can all agree that what our world needs are people who are happy, wise, discerning, and courageous. We can all agree that we need individuals who are good citizens, good parents, and good leaders. The question is, What produces this type of person? What are the character traits we can see in this type of person's life? Throughout history, philosophers and theologians have attempted to create a "map" of the moral life, pointing out those qualities which mark a person of character. Just as we need a map to navigate the complexities of a network of freeways, so we need a map to navigate the complexity of our daily lives. The planned destination at the end of our journey is that we find we are people of character. What's surprising as we examine the writings of the past is how much general agreement there is on what constitutes a truly virtuous individual.

The development of moral virtues in our lives is something greater than merely a concern with "values." All the current discussion over "family values" tends to play into the hands of the moral relativists. *Value* is a morally neutral term which identifies a preference. Virtue, on the other hand, is a quality of character which leads to action. All too often, values are something we argue about; virtue is a way of living. The contemporary philosopher James Q. Wilson, in his book, *The Moral Sense*, argues that instead of talking about "family values," we would be better off talking about the virtues that a decent family tries to inculcate.[1] All too often, our moral zeal is a matter of words rather than something we practice. So, if we want to practice the virtues and teach them to our children, we must understand what they are and what they look like in practice.

One of the greatest of all moral teachers was Aristotle. He thought long and hard about moral virtues and boiled them down to a list of what we now call the four "cardinal virtues"—fortitude, temperance, justice, and prudence. Aristotle felt that a balance of these four qualities would make for a truly moral individual. The word *cardinal* comes from a Latin word meaning "the hinge of a door." And these pivotal virtues open the door to moral strength. To Aristotle's four cardinal virtues, early Christian thinkers added three more, usually referred to as the "theological virtues"—faith, hope, and love. We call them "theological" because they are rooted in the character of God (*theos*). They are also called theological to differentiate them from Aristotle's virtues, ones that even pagans and unbelievers could practice. To these seven I'd like to add two more—compassion and humility. These nine qualities may not give us an exhaustive picture of morality, but they do give us a vision of moral character in action. They are, if you will, our road map to the destination of character.

Defining the Virtues

Let's briefly define these qualities as a step in the direction toward creating a moral map for our children.

Fortitude

Fortitude is moral courage, the strength to persevere and do the right thing in the face of adversity or challenge. We have no guarantee that doing the right thing will make us comfortable, successful, or even happy. In fact, doing the right thing is often costly to our immediate happiness. Ask the martyrs of old if standing up courageously is easy. Ask Wilberforce, who stood up against the slave trade. Ask Thomas More, who stood up for his own conscience against the command of his king (his story is powerfully told in the film *A Man for All Seasons*). Ask Dietrich Bonhoeffer, a brilliant theologian and pastor who died at the hands of the Nazis.

Fortitude is the ability to "hang in there!" even when doing the right thing extracts a price. It is the ability to courageously obey the dictates of our conscience rather than follow expediency or comfort. Life presents us with many temptations; fortitude is the ability to keep on doing the right thing no matter what the immediate consequences.

Temperance

Temperance is self-discipline. It is the ability to control our appetites and passions, to say no to the excess in our lives, and to live in moderation. Much of the unhappiness in our lives and in the world around us arises from our inability to control ourselves. When we lack temperance we lose control of our lives. But when we are temperate, we can keep our desires and appetites under the control of our reason and our knowledge of what is right and wrong.

We develop temperance primarily by forming good habits. If our habits are godly ones, they can teach us how to order our souls. They can train us to control our physical cravings and to ignore our culture's siren-song call to excess. The purpose of the world of advertising is to convince people that they need things which they really do not need. But as we develop temperance, we are able to resist these temporal pleasures in deference to eternal ones.

Justice

Justice is the virtue that enables us to treat one another fairly. There are two parts to justice. First, justice is rendering to others what we owe them. It is to take responsibility for paying our debts, whatever form that indebtedness might take. Justice is predicated upon honesty, upon keeping our promises.

Think what a different world this would be if people were truly concerned for others' needs and kept their promises to one another.

Second, justice involves treating others without unfair preference. It is equal punishment for identical offenses and equal rewards for identical merits. Children seem to have an innate sense of justice and are quick to point out to their parents when something "isn't fair." Justice looks beyond preferences and prejudices to treat all people as they deserve to be treated. Harmony within ourselves and with others is the natural reward of practicing justice.

Prudence

Prudence is taking care with the decisions one makes. While the imprudent person makes snap judgments and impulsive decisions, the prudent person weighs everything before making a decision. Prudence is practical wisdom which arises from paying close attention to what one has learned from one's life experiences and what one might gain from seeking wise counsel. Prudence manifests itself in real insight, the kind which marked Solomon when he wrote the Proverbs. It is making decisions with care, not being carried away with our emotions.

Prudence is not cleverness or calculation. It is not merely knowledge, but it is the ability to see clearly into a situation and act in the way that will ultimately bring about the best result.

Faith

Faith is the first of the three theological virtues. It is the realization of our need for something beyond us, the understanding that we cannot function on our own strength. Fundamentally it is saying yes to God, trusting that we can surrender our lives into His hands because He knows what's best for us. Hebrews chapter 11 gives us a roll call of the saints who practiced this virtue, men and women who stepped out beyond what they could see to follow the call of God.

We cannot reduce faith to intellectual knowledge. Faith is our ultimate allegiance to the personal loving God who has redeemed us and is committed to making us new creatures.

Hope

Hope is the virtue that keeps reminding us that the final chapter of our lives is not yet written. Hope looks beyond the sometimes vexing circumstances of life to see the hand of God at work in our lives. Hope is the ability to see with God's eyes, from His perspective, and therefore, never give up.

The New Testament points to our citizenship in heaven. Hope means we never need despair. The Father who loves us will see us through. The final chapter cannot be written prematurely for God has a purpose and plan for our lives. We need this confidence to get us through the struggles life inevitably brings. As Peter Kreeft has written, "Hope is like headlights. It is not easy to drive without headlights in the dark."[2]

Love

Love, says 1 Corinthians 13, is the greatest of the virtues. It is the center around which all the others move. Love, despite what our culture sometimes teaches us through popular music and film, is not just warm feelings or erotic attraction. Love is the ability to act toward others with sacrificial disregard for ourselves. Love is not just a feeling but an action. Jesus Christ's death on the cross for our sins is the ultimate illustration of true love. Loves gives its all for the benefit of the one who is loved.

Love is not abstract but practical and real. Many find it easy to commit themselves to the abstract mass of humanity. It is entirely a different matter to lay your own desires aside to provide practical love to your neighbor. As one old wag put it, "I love humanity; it's just human beings I can't stand!" True Christian love is not practiced to an abstract mob but to living, needy human individuals.

Humility

Humility is the virtue of seeing ourselves as we truly are. For many, humility is suspect as a virtue. They think of humility as a self-loathing reticence to assert oneself. But this is not humility. Real humility is not self-deprecation but an awareness of our finiteness and sinfulness. Humility is the knowledge of how limited and self-absorbed we really are. To be humble is to be realistic about our true condition. Its opposite, pride, keeps us at arm's length from others and does not allow us to be honest with ourselves and with God.

"Blessed are the poor in spirit," Jesus said. One translation has rendered this, "Blessed are those who know their need of God." This is true humility. It accepts the fact that the only accolades worth pursuing are those which come from our Father in heaven.

Compassion

The last of the virtues is compassion. Compassion means to feel with others, to be aware of the reality of other people and their needs. It is to exercise your imagination, that you might allow yourself to be touched by what touches them.

We must learn to put ourselves in the place of others, to be active and supportive because we can imagine what it might be like to be in their place. We are so naturally self-centered that true compassion is a rare and delightful virtue.

Rousseau said, "Compassion is a natural feeling, which, by moderating the violence of love of self in each individual, contributes to the preservation of the whole species. It is this compassion that hurries us without reflection to the relief of those who are in distress." Compassion recognizes the possibility that we could easily find ourselves experiencing the same distress as another, and therefore reaches out with all the passion of our hearts. Compassion recognizes that the down-and-out, the homeless, the starving, and the struggling all share a common humanity. Compassion causes us to experience the love that God has for them in their hurting circumstances.

Practicing the Virtues

These definitions can give us some idea of what the virtues look like. But to teach our children these definitions is not enough. Aristotle wisely believed that these virtues could not be taught as an academic exercise. They cannot just be learned about from a textbook. A merely intellectual understanding is insufficient. The moral virtues can only be attained through practicing them. A man stood in the middle of Times Square with a violin case tucked under his arm, looking lost and confused. He flagged down a police officer and asked, "How do you get to Carnegie Hall?" The policeman just smiled and said, "Practice, man, practice." There are no shortcuts to moral virtue. As Aristotle wrote, "We become just by doing just acts, temperate by doing temperate acts, brave by doing brave acts." As parents we must create an environment where moral actions are talked about, seen and imitated.

Good kids gone bad . . . we all know stories of children raised in good homes, where high moral standards were practiced and expected, who, when they reach adolescence or are out on their own, surrender themselves to moral vice. What is a parent to do if Aristotle is right and morality cannot be taught?

The very fact that many children go "off the rails" is an indication that the values and virtues taught in some homes never really take root in the soul. Values can be taken on secondhand and practiced under duress. But such children fail to catch a vision for the virtuous life, never have their moral imagination fully awakened. When this happens, parents should not beat themselves up or blame themselves unduly. We do the best we know how. One of the most godly men I have ever known had a daughter whom all the other youth in the church looked up to as a paragon of virtue. Her life was so seemingly spotless it was almost scary to be around her. In every area she followed the moral rules and sometimes even exceeded the rules in her zeal for holy living. She was a child that her parents were proud of . . . until she reached late adolescence. Suddenly, everything changed. She ended up getting pregnant and running away to marry the boy. Her parents were devastated.

We know that "God has no grandchildren," that we cannot be born into a secondhand experience of salvation. Each of us must have our own relationship with the heavenly Father. It is the same with ethics. Obedience to secondhand rules does not make us moral people. Your children cannot live off of your moral capital.

What, then, is a parent to do? Romans teaches us that God has placed a moral law in the heart of every person. Our sinful nature puts pressure on us to transgress this law. We must resist the tendency to indoctrinate our children into slavish obedience to moral platitudes. Instead, we can work with God to awaken within them their capacity for moral action. We do this by giving them a vision of what a truly moral life is like.

Let's face it. This is not an easy world in which to practice moral virtue. Our children need all the help they can get. In the chapters that follow I want to share with you some of the things that can help you foster the moral imagination. These are not the guaranteed "ten steps to a moral child." Instead, they are suggestions for building the kind of environment in your home and family which will best allow moral virtue and meaningful faith to grow.

Train a child in the way he should go, and when he is old he will not turn from it.

—Proverbs 22:6

Moral virtue comes about as the result of habit.

—Aristotle

If you want a man to keep his head when the crisis comes you must give him some training before it comes.

—Seneca

•   •   •

4

Making a Habit of Virtue

---

*Moral Virtue
and Habit Formation*

---

*W*e've all experienced it: the struggle to overcome bad habits. There is something about habits that can produce a stranglehold on us. Ask anyone who has ever tried to break an addiction like smoking or drinking. Exercise of willpower rarely suffices. To break a bad habit, we must replace it with a better one. This is why many ex-smokers reach for a pack of gum.

Our children may have good intentions but experience great difficulty in seeing these intentions through. The bare application of willpower is simply not enough to help them overcome the nagging behaviors that trip them up. It takes great effort, steady application, and strength of will to make real changes in one's life. Our sentiments must be educated, training the heart and the mind together. As the Scriptures state, from childhood we must learn to love good and abhor evil. The modern nonjudgmental attitude of values clarification will not suffice to make our children the kind of people God wants them to be. They must learn the right thing and build habits that help them follow through.

Much of the difficulty comes in making decisions. Because our children are faced with multitudinous decisions every day, they can become overwhelmed with the stress of constantly trying to make the right ones. Part of the business of moral education is reducing the number of decisions that children need to make by inculcating in them patterns of habit which naturally and instinctively help them choose the right course of action. They will live most of their lives by instinctual habits, making it imperative that these habits be good ones.

Getting in a Good Rut

When I was young, everyone in my family owned motorcycles. These were not the huge motorcycles you see cruising down the freeway; they were "trail bikes"—small-engined cycles we would strap into the back of our pickup and take up into the Oregon mountains. There, we would explore old logging roads, tracing them through the green and beautiful forests. One thing which marked these old roads were the ruts, worn deep into the now-dry earth by huge logging trucks. Sometimes we would slip our bikes down into these ruts and let them take us where they would. But once we tired of this, it was always a bit of a struggle to get the bikes out of the ruts because they were worn so deeply. Habits are ruts worn deep down into our consciousness; they are paths imbedded in our lives through frequent repetition. Polite manners, hygiene, control of our appetites—these are all worthwhile ruts. Habits. But many habits are bad for us. Through frequent capitulation to our baser cravings and self-centeredness, we often wear grooves that we can only overcome by replacing them with good habits.

We cannot leave our children to their human natures, for these natures are fallen and will often lead them in the wrong direction. We would never allow our children to follow their natural instincts in the brushing of their teeth. If we did, their teeth would surely all decay and fall out. Instead, we instruct them in the importance of good dental hygiene and then make sure they practice it. How, then, could we ever leave them to themselves in the area of morality? Their moral hygiene is of pressing importance. It's true that their natures will lead them astray, but we must instruct our children in spite of their nature. If we are in the habit of doing the wrong thing, doing the right thing becomes almost impossible. "Can the Ethiopian change his skin or the leopard its spots? Neither can you do good who are accustomed to doing evil" (Jeremiah 13:23). We must help our children overcome their bondage to patterns of fallen behavior. We must teach them to control their nature.

We can most effectively teach our children to become moral people by teaching them good habits. Aristotle defined *habit* as "second nature." It is a replacement for the old, natural ways of doing things. When a good habit becomes fixed in our lives, it will crowd out a bad instinctual one. "Habit," says Charlotte Mason, "forces nature into new channels."[1] It is a powerful reality to know that as we develop good habits we can literally transform our instincts and reflexes.

Habits get us beyond relying on feelings to produce good behavior. We cannot rely on feelings and moods to help us live our lives. They can, too often, lead us in the wrong direction. We may not feel like being obedient, kind, or discerning. If we are relying on feelings of love to help us act kindly, we will too often find ourselves instead acting short-tempered and self-centered. We think and act according to the ruts we have grooved in our brains and in our patterns of behavior. When we set deep grooves in our lives with good habits, our tendency is to respond in the right way. We can and must learn new reflexes.

An athlete must give himself to much practice if he wants to excel at his chosen sport. The ability to smash a home run out beyond center field, to consistently sink baskets from behind the three-point line, to throw a 75-yard pass which arrives at pinpoint accuracy, to stroke a golf ball 150 yards to within a few feet of the pin—none of these abilities come automatically. Sure, you or I might on occasion be able to perform one of these feats, but to do so with the kind of regularity that a professional athlete manages requires commitment to practice. Skill comes through practice. As a pro golfer said with a glint in his eye after chipping his ball into the cup from well off the putting surface: "It's amazing how lucky you get when you practice this several hours a day!" Virtue, like a sport, must be practiced until it becomes habitual. Like the basketball player who must sink the free throws with only a second left in the game, we must build good habits into our lives so that we can respond virtuously when the "crunch time" comes. Moral principles are of little good if you cannot put them into practice in the face of a difficult moral test.

The moral virtues mentioned in the last chapter are only made a part of our lives when we practice them to such a degree that they become a replacement for our natural tendencies. We call this process by the biblical term *sanctification*. Sanctification is the process by which we are transformed into the character of Jesus, our ultimate model of moral virtue. Of course we will never practice the virtues perfectly and will always stand in need of God's forgiveness, but growth in character is developed as the practice of the virtues becomes more natural due to the formation of good habits. If we can help our children develop a vision for goodness, then they will desire good things because "right desires" are etched deep into their hearts. If we can re-educate their passions, then, when times of stress and temptation arise, our children will fall back on the good habits they have developed.

We need to see ourselves as our children's allies in the overcoming of bad habits and the formation of good ones. We should be cheerleaders rather than policemen. We should emphasize the joys of moral living rather than always "laying down the law" in such a way that it seems impossibly burdensome.

Building Good Habits

There is no quick and easy method for building character into our children's lives. There are, however, some practical ways to help your children develop a strong moral character.

1. Catch your children being good and praise them for it. Praise is a strong way to reinforce any action. Our children's peers often "praise" them for unruly or bad behavior. Much of the television and film fare our children take in reinforces bad behaviors by making them seem "cool" or independent or "with it." We can best counter this with praise for good behavior; they need to see that moral behavior is also noticed and applauded. Make them feel proud of themselves for choosing the right thing.

2. Discuss various moral scenarios which your children may face. Over a meal, at bedtime, or on a trip, make up a story which presents a specific kind of moral dilemma; finding money, being asked by a good friend to do something wrong, finding it more comfortable to lie in a situation than to tell the truth. Create the whole scenario so that they can picture it in their minds, and then explore with them various options and possible responses. Clearly and gently guide them to the right path. Let them discover the right answer themselves by asking them questions and pointing out the flaws in sinful responses to the dilemma. If they have explored the possibilities and consequences of certain actions in advance, they will be better prepared to make the right decision if such a situation should arise. Working out the response ahead of time will make doing the right thing more automatic.

3. Teach your children to "filter" what they see, hear, and read. It is inevitable that they will at some time see and hear negative messages through television, movies, or the books they read. You can use these opportunities to sharpen their moral skills and as a forum for discussing the merits and demerits of the questions raised by the negative message. Teach them to be justly skeptical, that they do not have to

believe everything they're told. Discuss portrayals, consequences, and presuppositions (we'll discuss this term in the next chapter) that come to them through entertainment and education. This will help them to "think Christianly." Use every opportunity to hone this important skill.

4. Be a moral example to your children. As we discussed in an earlier chapter, your most powerful tool for teaching morality is your own life. You can be a living example of morality and virtue in action. Be ruthlessly honest with yourself as you examine your own life; an evasion of right action can send a powerful contradictory message if you're preaching morality. Of course, you will fail and fall short at times, but strive to practice what you preach.

5. Discuss the moral virtues with your children. Using the previous chapter as a jumping-off place, do some serious thinking and studying about the moral virtues. Try to work out clear definitions for yourself which you can then teach to your children. Go to history and to the Scriptures for examples to emulate. As a family, study the character qualities in these examples and start a project that will help you develop them in your family. You could focus on one each month; everyone looks for examples and opportunities to develop that particular virtue. Let your kids see that you, too, are a learner in the school of the virtues.

6. Use stories to emphasize moral qualities to your children. Stories are one of your most powerful tools if you wish your children to grow deeper in the virtues. In chapter 13 we will discuss how you can use stories to effectively teach morality.

7. Memorize short sayings, scriptures, or mottoes which reinforce your children's good behavior. Give them short, memorable phrases that they can use to come to grips with moral living and can draw upon in times of temptation. Phrases like:

"Honesty is the best policy."

"Trust in the Lord with all your heart and lean not on your own understanding."

"Haste makes waste."

These phrases are easy to remember and will remind them of the right thing to do and say in a difficult situation. These short bits of wisdom help us to dig ruts of righteous thinking into our brains. Find such snippets of wisdom and post them where everyone can see them and learn them.

Morality is never an easy or automatic thing to build into our children's lives. And while we cannot teach it as an academic subject, there is much we can do to make it a powerful part of our children's lives. In addition to the ideas discussed above, there are two other essential components of moral education.

The first is that we must teach our children to think like Christians. If it is true that our actions are in large measure influenced by the way we think, we must learn to think correctly, to "think Christianly." We must help our children to understand their faith and its meaning if it is to influence their lives. Sometimes we can give the impression that faith is primarily an emotional experience and neglect to show them how it changes our intellectual understanding of the world around us. In the next section of this book, you will find some tools you can use to help your child develop a Christian mind— an understanding of theology and of their Christian heritage and how to relate this to their knowledge of an increasingly secular world. We will conclude the second part of this book with some practical things you can do to foster your children's spiritual life.

The second essential component is the environment we create for our children. To be responsible in this area means asking some hard questions about issues like television and music and knowing how to utilize such things as the arts, reading, and sports to build an appreciation for beauty, truth, and fairness. This discussion will make up the third part of the book.

Let me close this first section with a reminder that it is only through the grace of God, and our exercising of that same kind of grace to our children, that any development in our own character or that of our children can take place. All true change takes place only through Him who has promised to make us a new creation. Ultimately, we are His work, but He gives us a part in the process by asking us to practice three things: self-discipline, commitment, and love. Any moral change starts and ends with Him, but must include these three elements on our part.

PART TWO

The Christian Mind and Spirit

My people are destroyed from lack of knowledge.

—Hosea 4:6

•   •   •

5

Thinking Christianly

*Christianity as a Way of Thinking
as Well as a Way of Life*

 $\mathcal{D}$ addy, who made God?"

"Mommy, how do fish breathe in the water? Why don't they drown?"

"Where does the 'fluff' in my belly button come from?"

Kids learn about their world by asking questions. Lots of questions. Sometimes we wish that the questions didn't come so thick and fast, but this is the way kids learn.

We are all natural question-askers. Observe any child at about five years old and you'll see the evidence of our inborn tendency to ask questions: "Why?" "How?" "What?" "When?" The questions flow forth as naturally as water from a spring. As we grow older, we learn that people don't like us to ask too many questions, especially the uncomfortable kind that don't lend themselves to easy answers. And so we learn to bottle up our inquisitiveness, suppress our longing for answers, and live without any real expectation of the solutions to life's mysteries. We lose the wide-eyed, open-minded, questioning attitude of the child.

Someone has said that a philosopher is one who asks questions that the rest of us don't think to ask. Or perhaps the philosopher's questions are ones that the rest of us have forgotten how to ask; we are often too busy earning our daily bread, keeping ourselves busy, and meeting the immediate needs of the moment to ask about the meaning of life, the nature of truth, and the health of our souls. Though too many of our modern philosophers idle their time away with minutiae and concentrate on much less grand and important questions, these issues of the soul have traditionally been the province of the philosopher. For the philosopher is the one who loves (*philo*) wisdom (*sophia*). The theologian is much the same as the philosopher, asking questions about the matters we all too often take for granted.

Ultimately, everyone is a theologian. We all have opinions and ideas about God and how we are to relate to Him. We develop these ideas and opinions in one of two ways: With our hearts open to the truth, we give ourselves to conscious and careful thought and study, or, instead, we take someone else's word (a family member, a friend, a Sunday school teacher, a pastor) as truth without investigating it. Many people develop their conceptions of life in the same way that they catch a cold. They breathe in the "germs" of ideas out of the cultural air around them. They are exposed to an idea or opinion, and unless they can immediately think of a rebuttal or know that the idea contradicts the opinion of someone whose authority they hold more dear, the idea "becomes their own." And it never ceases to amaze me how vociferously someone will argue for opinions which they have barely thought through for themselves.

Many of us, if we are honest, expect our kids to believe everything we tell them without questioning. Now, this attitude is serviceable when a child is six and believes that Mom and Dad are an inexhaustible fountain of wisdom. As he grows older, however, he learns the truth—the dreadful, fearful, and humbling truth: Mom and Dad do not know everything. About the time he begins to sprout pimples and develop acne, this attitude usually transforms from "Mom and Dad don't know everything" to "Mom and Dad don't know anything!" In the teen years our kids struggle to find their own identities as individuals. It is at this time that the beliefs and opinions of their parents will come under scrutiny.

When this moment in time comes, the pressures of school, peers, and the media may cause your teens to question all that you have held true and important. Because so many teens have not learned how to think clearly as Christians, they may have positive feelings about their faith, a warm and fuzzy sense of love for God, but they lack understanding of how their faith affects the way they see the great issues of life. And so one of two things happens: Either the young person puts his spiritual life into a separate compartment from the "real things" of life, in which case his faith becomes irrelevant and inconsequential, or he rejects the teachings of his parents as old-fashioned, outdated, and false. But such a dreary outcome is much less likely if a child is raised as a truth-seeker and a question-asker, and if the parents have provided that child with an intellectual framework for viewing life which reflects a biblical faith. As our children grow older, it is so important that they begin to come to a clear understanding of Christianity as *the truth*.

We can help our children develop a passion for the truth. Now, many parents would settle for having children who agreed with them on most of life's essentials. Parenting can often take the form of a benevolent sort of brainwashing, indoctrinating children with the truth as the parent sees it. The parent's motives may be pure, but if children are to develop in their relationship with God, growing deep in character and in faith, they must do it for themselves. They must develop a Christian perspective of the world.

We can call this Christian perspective our "worldview." By worldview, we mean the set of presuppositions we have about the world and our lives. We use these assumptions when we do any thinking at all, and they play a powerful part in shaping the way we look at life. For example, those who hold to the materialist worldview have the presupposition that nothing is real except what they can see or touch. This is the worldview of the astronomer Carl Sagan who says that the only thing that has ever existed is the universe. If this materialist presupposition is true, then God, whom we cannot see or touch or interrogate with our questions, could not exist. Now, neither Sagan nor anybody else can ever prove that God does not exist, since this information is simply not available to the senses alone. For the materialist, however, this belief is the basis for other beliefs—in other words, a presupposition. If you hold this presupposition, then any other data which comes your way is interpreted through the grid of this presupposition.

Therefore, when the materialist gets a glimpse of the wonderful order and beauty of the universe, he does not draw the obvious conclusion—that a divine power, which exists outside the universe, brought the universe into existence and sustains it. Instead, the materialist makes creative mental leaps, which require an unbelievable amount of faith, to draw the conclusion that the universe is the result of chance, that somehow chaos itself has produced order. And so, because of the difference in presuppositions, the Christian and the materialist draw different conclusions about the existence of evil, the nature of man, and the future of our world.

If our children, then, are to think like Christians, they must understand the presuppositions which underlie the Christian worldview and capture a glimpse of Christianity as the most coherent and clear explanation of the world we live in. If our children have instead a mixture of Christian and non-Christian presuppositions, the result will be confusion, probably leading to error.

It all starts with asking questions. Just as a body of water becomes stagnant when it does not find release into a stream or river, so will the souls and minds of our children become stagnant if we do not encourage them to ask the questions of life.

The Need for Thinking Christianly

A coherent worldview is crucial for developing the kind of Christian faith that can stand strong against the pressures of our modern world. There are several reasons for this.

1. It is a defense against "creeping secularism." The attitudes and beliefs which undermine biblical teachings and standards did not just suddenly appear in our society and garner immediate acceptance. Instead, the influence of secularism has been slow and insidious. It has crept into the consciousness of even Christian believers because some do not clearly understand the Christian worldview well enough to detect the slow erosion by the inroads of unbelieving presuppositions. Someone has said that the best defense is a good offense. This is certainly the case in the intellectual realm. If our kids understand the content of their faith as a unified view of the world, the lure of other worldviews will be much less powerful.

2. We can help strengthen others in their commitment to their faith. Not everyone is gifted in the same way intellectually, and we must use those gifts God has given us to help others grow strong. Many fellow believers will not have the opportunity to develop the kind of understanding which strengthens them against the attacks of those who would challenge their faith. C. S. Lewis wrote about the duty of Christian intellectuals to encourage their brothers and sisters in Christ to develop a clearly Christian philosophy as a response to the challenges of modern life:

> To be ignorant and simple now—not to be able to meet the enemies on their own ground—would be to throw down our weapons, and to betray our uneducated brethren who have, under God, no defense but us against the

> intellectual attacks of the heathen. Good philosophy
> must exist, if for no other reason, because bad philos-
> ophy needs to be answered. . . . The learned life then is,
> in some sense, a duty.[1]

If this was true of the time when Lewis wrote this essay, it is
doubly true of our time. While not every child could or should
aspire to be a "Christian intellectual," certainly a goal worth
pursuing is that every child could grow up to be an intellectual
Christian.

3. It honors God when we use well what He has given us.
Our intellectual capabilities are a gift from God and we honor
Him when we develop them. Jesus defined the first and greatest commandment as loving God "with all your heart and with
all your soul and with all your mind" (Matthew 22:37,38).
What does the last part of this triad mean, to love God with our
mind? Certainly it means disciplining our minds to see life
from God's perspective, having the humility to know the limits
of our reason, training our minds to look to God for guidance.
Loving God with all our mind means doing all our thinking to
the glory of God. A mind so conditioned is a mind that will
bring about changes in us. As Paul wrote in Romans 12:1, "Be
transformed by the renewing of your mind." True change
comes through not only changing our heart, but also through
allowing God to change our mind.

4. Thinking Christianly helps us to more effectively
share the gospel. "Always be prepared to give an answer to
everyone who asks you to give the reason for the hope that you
have," writes the apostle Peter (1 Peter 3:15). Some Christians
find themselves unable to articulate the meaning of the gospel
because their faith is based upon their feelings alone; they can
only rely on the telling of their personal experience. Now, the
use of personal testimony in sharing the gospel is an important
factor. But if we fail to back it up with a clear explanation of the
meaning behind our experiences, we are simply asking people
to join with us in the "good feelings" that relationship with
Christ can produce. But the gospel is more than good feelings
or positive experiences. It is the truth.

It is only when we know the gospel as the truth that we can help others catch a vision of the truth, or respond to those whose vision of the truth is different than ours. Hindus, Jehovah's Witnesses, sun worshipers, and atheists all have good feelings from time to time as a result of their beliefs. But we must be prepared to demonstrate with our intellect as well as with our hearts and lives that the good news of Jesus Christ is the only true hope for a fallen humanity. It takes effort to make our testimony intellectually compelling as well as emotionally satisfying. Oh, what a gift to our children if we can help them understand and articulate with clarity the hope of the gospel, if we can teach them how to think Christianly.

A Biblical Defense of Christian Thinking

Some believers have mistakenly concluded that the life of faith is somehow antithetical to the life of the mind, that using reason is somehow unspiritual or shows lack of spiritual maturity. Actually the opposite is true. The Bible clearly points out the need for Christians to exercise their intellects in the pursuit of spiritual growth. There are four biblical reasons why Christians need to be thinkers:

First, God created us as rational beings and gives us direction that requires us to think. We are called to use our reason wisely.

> "Come now, let us reason together," says the Lord (Isaiah 1:18).

> Brothers, stop thinking like children. In regard to evil be infants, but in your thinking be adults (1 Corinthians 14:20).

Second, God's revelation is rational. God did not leave us alone to make guesses and conjectures about His nature and His purposes. Instead He communicated to us through the mode of rational discourse. The words of Christ in Scripture include argument, clarification, and appeal to reason. (See, for example, the Sermon on the Mount).

Third, we are held responsible for the knowledge we are given. God expects us to use the intellectual tools we have to respond appropriately to His Word.

> For since the creation of the world God's invisible qualities—His eternal power and divine nature—have been clearly seen, being understood from what has been made, so that men are without excuse (Romans 1:20).

Lastly, we must cooperate with God in His goal for our minds so that they can be renewed by His grace and power, becoming tools that will empower rather than hinder us in the walk of faith.

> Therefore, I urge you, brothers, in view of God's mercy, to offer your bodies as living sacrifices, holy and pleasing to God—this is your spiritual act of worship. Do not conform any longer to the pattern of this world, but be transformed by the renewing of your mind (Romans 12:1,2).

Ultimately, thinking theologically is important because our way of thinking is not merely something abstract; it influences the very way we live our lives. Psychologists expend a great deal of effort in trying to change the perceptions of their patients because they know that what a person thinks influences the way that person behaves. Our perceptions of ourselves, others, and our world have a powerful influence on our mental health and on our ability to function well in society. The same is true in theology—wrong thinking results in wrong action. In Romans, the apostle Paul addresses those Christians whose incorrect concept of grace and forgiveness was such that it gave them a license to live without any sort of moral restraint. Not understanding the nature of God's mercy, some of the Roman believers had used their misunderstanding to justify sinful lifestyles.

Similarly, in his epistles the apostle John battled the ideas of the Gnostics. The Gnostics believed that only the spiritual realm was important and that one could reach such a level of spiritual maturity that the actions of the body would cease to matter. This gave them permission to indulge their bodily lusts as they pleased. Since their theology told them that immorality in the body did not corrupt their spirits, much of their lifestyle was licentious rather than disciplined.

Also, the belief in an impending millennium caused many believers in the year A.D. 1000 to take to the hills to await the coming of Christ. They neglected their jobs and responsibilities because their set of beliefs (theology) led them to expect that Christ would return soon enough to make all the other activities of life irrelevant.

The contemporary conflict over the question of abortion is one more example of how belief affects action. Everyone has a different perception of what constitutes human life, what a "right" is, and the value and worth of human life, both born and unborn. The differing perceptions lie at the root of all the rhetoric and accusation on both sides. The only way one side can ever convince the other side is to change the other's theology of humanity.

The Boldness of Intelligent Belief

Perhaps the underlying reason many believers fail to give high priority to the life of the mind is because they believe to do so would draw them away from a simple trust in God. It is easy to see how they could draw this conclusion. When we look to the bastions of intellectual knowledge, our colleges and universities, we find a distressing reality. Faith seems dead in the academic community. Those thinkers in our great universities who hold to a biblical perspective of the world are indeed a small minority. In the face of the overwhelming onslaught of unbelief in the intellectual world, it is hardly surprising that many Christians have come to the conclusion that the mind is more an ally of secularism than of the Christian faith.

You've probably heard it many times, and perhaps you've said it yourself: "I don't want to complicate matters. I just hold to the simple gospel." While there is some truth and nobility in this statement, we must be careful that it doesn't become an excuse for intellectual laziness when it comes to searching out the things of God. There is a vast difference between being simple and being simplistic. We are simplistic when we adopt that feeling of pride that says it is unnecessary for us to be schooled further in the truth. We are simplistic when we reduce the grand message of the Bible into a few convenient formulas. We are simplistic when we cut ourselves off from the riches that come from intense study and fervent prayer.

To be simple, on the other hand, is to grasp hold of the essentials of the faith and to realize that ultimately it all comes down to opening our hearts to God's forgiveness and the Lordship of Christ in our daily lives. But what we will find when we give ourselves to study and thinking is that the awesome simplicity of the truth is only enriched. Only those who have grappled with the depths of meaning in the atonement of Christ will fully appreciate what was accomplished on the cross. Only those who have struggled with the paradox of grace and responsibility will fully know how much God has done for us and how much He desires to do through us.

Christians have no reason to be intellectually ashamed or embarrassed. The Christian worldview is a strong and logical answer to our culture's search for meaning. Our beliefs will stand up both in the court of reason and in the court of experience. The Christian worldview is the only fully satisfying way to answer the questions men have struggled with throughout history. We have, as a later chapter will attempt to demonstrate, a rich heritage of clear, creative, and incisive thought which has characterized the church down through the ages. We can stand toe-to toe with the secularists in the intellectual sphere. We have nothing to fear from the search for truth because Jesus Christ said that He was the truth.

Let no one fool you into thinking that the secularist owns the intellectual high ground. It is the secularist's worldview that is riddled with contradictions and blind faith. Many fine books have been written pointing out these problems, a handful of which I have recommended in the list at the end of the next chapter. But one of the most succinct and powerful statements is the tongue-in-cheek poem by Steve Turner, "Creed," which purports to be a recitation of our society's set of beliefs.

CREED

We believe in Marxfreudanddarwin.
We believe everything is OK.
as long as you don't hurt anyone,
to the best of your definition of hurt,
and to the best of your knowledge.

We believe in sex before during
and after marriage.
We believe in the therapy of sin.
We believe that adultery is fun.
We believe that sodomy's OK.
We believe that taboos are taboo.

We believe that everything's getting better
despite evidence to the contrary.
The evidence must be investigated.
You can prove anything with evidence.

We believe there's something in horoscopes,
UFO's and bent spoons;
Jesus was a good man just like Buddha
Mohammed and ourselves.
He was a good moral teacher although we think
his good morals were bad.

We believe that all religions are basically the same,
at least the one that we read was.
They all believe in love and goodness.
They only differ on matters of
creation sin heaven hell God and salvation.

We believe that after death comes The Nothing
because when you ask the dead what happens
they say Nothing.
If death is not the end, if the dead have lied,
then it's compulsory heaven for all
excepting perhaps Hitler, Stalin and Genghis Khan.

We believe in Masters and Johnson.
What's selected is average.
What's average is normal.
What's normal is good.

We believe that man is essentially good.
It's only his behavior that lets him down.
This is the fault of society.
Society is the fault of conditions.
Conditions are the fault of society.

We believe that each man must find the truth
that is right for him.
Reality will adjust accordingly.
The universe will readjust. History will alter.

We believe that there is no absolute truth
excepting the truth that there is no absolute truth.

We believe in the rejection of creeds.[2]

Turner has quite effectively pointed to some of the contradictions within modern thought, humorously skewering the irrational beliefs that our modern society holds so dear. Contrary to the illogic in secular presuppositions, the Christian worldview is rational, coherent, and provides answers to the deepest of human questions.

Theology is the act of the believing person reflecting upon his belief and studying it methodically in order to reach a deeper understanding of God's revelation and to surrender himself more fully and more intelligently to God's manifest will and plan of salvation in the contemporary world.

—Thomas Merton

Theology is "that discipline which strives to give a coherent statement of the doctrines of the Christian faith, based primarily on the Scriptures, placed in the context of culture in general, worded in contemporary idiom, and related to issues of life."

—Millard J. Erickson

• • •

6

Every Child a Theologian

*Seeing the World
Through Biblical Eyes*

*I*n our age of microchips, microprocessors, and microwave ovens, the study of theology strikes many people as a pursuit that is at best eccentric, at worst escapist, and usually, completely irrelevant. To think of lives devoted to such a task is seen as a waste of human intelligence by the average unbeliever. And even in the church, many feel that the study of theology is anything but an essential part of the Christian life. Those who study such issues as God's character, attributes, and actions are, by some odd twist of values, seen as focusing on minutiae. To those on the theological left, God is so completely beyond our human understanding that any attempt to unravel the mysteries of His person and will is viewed as a foolhardy pursuit. Those on the right wing are often so caught up in their own spiritual ecstasies (or in the pursuit of those ecstasies) that they have little time or patience to think more deeply about the intellectual framework of their faith.

Is Theology Unspiritual?

In fact, some Christians believe the pursuit of theological questions to be an unspiritual activity. To search out the "whys" of our faith is seen as evidence of a lack of simple trust in God. To this kind of Christian, throwing all thought to the wind and relying on an experiential relationship with God is seen as a badge of spiritual maturity. Dorothy L. Sayers, with tongue firmly planted in cheek, reveals this attitude in a frighteningly accurate catechism:

Q: What is faith?

A: Resolutely shutting your eyes to scientific fact.

Q: What is the human intellect?

A: A barrier to faith.

Q: What are the seven Christian virtues?

A: Respectability; childishness; mental timidity; dullness; sentimentality; censoriousness; and depression of spirits.[1]

What is at the root of this negative attitude toward theology and the process of intellectually sorting out our belief system? Is it not, at its heart, that we choose to erect a defensive structure which allows us to hold firmly to what we believe rather than take the time and effort to examine the doubts and questions which assail us? Is it not a way of dealing with questions by not dealing with them? To simply believe without examination means we must place unquestioning trust in the belief systems of our pastors, parents, or spiritual leaders. It keeps us from stirring up uncomfortable disagreements or exposing ourselves to the tenuousness of some of our own most cherished conceptions. We can simply place our trust in another's understanding of our faith. But if we do this, is it really ours? As Sören Kierkegaard writes,

> There are many people who reach their conclusions about life like schoolboys; they cheat their master by copying the answer out of a book without having worked out the sum for themselves.[2]

Is it not the case that simple intellectual laziness is the great enemy of our attempt to make our faith really and truly our own? Is it not an elaborate evasion, building a spiritualized justification for what is really just laziness in the face of the truth? Surely this is not something we want to see either in our own lives or in those of our children.

The Dangers of Theological Ignorance

The dangers of theological ignorance are obvious to those who keep up on the latest movements in the Christian church. Thinly veiled secularism in the guise of psychology, irrational forms of fanaticism, or the gospel presented as the latest ticket to prosperity and success, mark our contemporary church. Without a concrete theological framework against which to measure the latest "innovations," many Christians are "blown here and there by every wind of teaching" (Ephesians 4:14), basing their belief systems on whoever has the most potent rhetoric or most charismatically tells them what they want to hear. Whatever tickles their ears or appeals to their lifestyle becomes the "truth."

If our goal in life is wealth and the prestige that money can buy, we will easily fall prey to those doctrines that promise us it is God's will for us to be rich. If we wish to live a lifestyle of sensual pleasure, we will follow a doctrinal system that gives us permission to live in that way. That is why Paul admonishes Titus on the importance of solid teaching as a foundational requirement for church leadership:

> He [the elder] must hold firmly to the trustworthy message as it has been taught, so that he can encourage others by sound doctrine and refute those who oppose it (Titus 1:9).

> You must teach what is in accord with sound doctrine (Titus 2:1).

Obviously, Paul would disagree with those who say that theology is an unimportant or unspiritual pursuit.

Let's face the truth. Everyone, consciously or not, is a theologian. You are. Your kids are. We all hold to a set of ideas about the meaning of our lives, our origin, our history, and our destiny. If we have not taken the time and effort to think through these questions for ourselves, we have drawn on the ideas of parents, teachers, books, the media, etc. We may not always live in perfect accordance with our beliefs, but we all hold beliefs. They may be primitive; they may be sophisticated. They may be deeply traditional; they may be radical. The issue is not whether we have beliefs and opinions, but whether our beliefs and opinions square with reality, with what is true.

I am not suggesting that a fully logical, comprehensive theological system is the ultimate achievement of the Christian life—far from it. Faith is not the rational assent to a theological system. Theology is not faith, and it does not precede faith. Theology fleshes faith out. Few people arrive at faith as the result of a lengthy philosophical search. Instead, theology is the way that we put intellectual flesh on the skeleton of faith. The medieval theologian Anselm wrote, "*Credo ut intellectum*"—I believe in order that I may understand. Once we find ourselves in the arena of faith, theology helps us understand our world and ourselves in a new way. If faith is, to some degree, a leap over a chasm of that which cannot fully be explained, theology is the attempt to build a bridge of understanding back over that chasm. As rational beings, we search for understanding. That is the way God made us.

We grow both in grace and in knowledge (Ephesians 4:15 and 2 Peter 3:18). Theology helps us make sense of the movements of grace in our lives, to grasp what God is doing in us and how we can cooperate with Him.

How Do We Do Theology?

Only a few people have the time, money, or inclination to get professional training in theology. So a theological education is not necessarily the answer to developing a deeper understanding of faith. There are actually some simple steps you can take that will help you begin to "think theologically" on your own. These steps will help you work out more clearly what you believe and serve as tools you can use to train your children in the basics as they grow older. There is no deep secret to doing theology. It starts very simply, by asking specific questions.

Ask Specific Questions

One way to learn is to ask questions. When your children ask you questions, especially somewhat thorny ones like "Who made God?" you are presented with the perfect opportunity to help them learn to think through a question from a Christian viewpoint.

In this particular instance, you have the opportunity to differentiate between God and human beings (that we are not eternally existent, as He is), to point to the nature of God's creative act (that He created *ex nihilo*—out of nothing) and to stand in awe and wonder of how great God is, and how reliant on Him we are. Asking questions provides the opportunity to think about things more deeply. As adults, if we can continue to ask questions, we can continue to learn.

No question is too stupid or abstract to be fodder for constructive thinking. Some make fun of theologians (especially medieval ones) by repeating the old question, "How many angels can dance on the head of a pin?" But when you think about it, you could learn a lot from asking such a seemingly silly question. For example: Do angels exist? What is the nature of angels? Are they material beings or spiritual beings? Do they take up space in our physical world when they operate in it? Would God command angels to dance on the head of a pin? Asking such questions should send the believer to the Scriptures to search out answers and increase understanding.

Study the Scriptures Carefully

The place to begin our thinking about theology is with the Bible. We know about God, not because of our marvelous human discoveries, but because of His revelation to us. It is never too soon to introduce our children to God's Word.

> From infancy you have known the holy Scriptures, which are able to make you wise for salvation through faith in Christ Jesus. All Scripture is God-breathed and is useful for teaching, rebuking, correcting and training in righteousness, so that the man of God may be thoroughly equipped for every good work (2 Timothy 3:15-17).

Paul calls Timothy to immerse himself in the Bible if he is to learn the ways of God and grow in faith. A solid knowledge of the Scriptures will "equip us for every good work." Scripture is both the plumb line by which we discern truth from error, and our source of strength for living the Christian life.

This kind of equipping, however, does not come from a casual acquaintance with the Bible. Those who take time to dig into the Scriptures, mining them for the truth, will take away the richest of ore. Acts 17:11 commends the Berean believers because they "examined the Scriptures every day." Examining is not the casual act of perusing a page. Rather, it is to come before the Scriptures with a heart that is seeking the truth, and a mind that is fully engaged in searching out the will of God.

The Bible is not a scrapbook of inspiring thoughts, a magical oracle of knowledge, or a source of quick-fix answers. It should be read carefully and studied in context. We must let it teach us and train us in God's ways. As with any other reading we do, we must interpret what is being said. Since it is the Word of God we are dealing with, it becomes doubly important to interpret it correctly.

Some Simple Rules for Interpreting the Bible

1. We must consider the context and the author's purpose when interpreting the meaning of a biblical statement and resist the tendency to look for hidden or secret meanings, or build elaborate schemes of thought based on symbolism. Whenever possible, we can accept the plain and obvious meaning as the correct one.

2. The meaning of a biblical statement fits the historical and cultural context of its writer and its original readers. We cannot impose our twentieth-century worldview upon it and try to force it to address issues it does not address.

3. The meaning of a passage is always consistent with the author's context in that particular book. Each book of the Bible has a specific message, which fits in with the overall message of the Bible. We must ask ourselves how each passage fits in with the message of each book.

4. The meaning of a passage of Scripture will not contradict the meaning of any other passage. Scripture harmonizes with Scripture. We need to discover the whole picture and interpret it Scripture by Scripture.

5. Extensive discussions of an issue take priority over brief allusions. When we're trying to develop an understanding of an issue, we need to focus on the passages where we find the most complete discussion of the issue, not where it is casually mentioned in the midst of another discussion.

6. A doctrinal discussion takes priority over any single instance of experience in a biblical narrative. Just because Jesus rubbed mud in the eyes of a blind man does not necessarily mean that this is the preferred method of healing.

7. We should make central what Scripture makes central and not let ourselves be led into doctrinal side issues that make

more for argumentation than growth. For an example, some Christians are preoccupied with the study of Bible prophecy. They spend too much time playing "pin the tail on the Antichrist," when their time would be better spent discovering how to "occupy till He comes."

If you are serious about doing biblical studies that are accurate and inspiring, I highly recommend the book by Kay Arthur entitled *How to Study Your Bible* (Harvest House, 1994). This book gets high marks for its clarity, usability, and simplicity and will help you improve your study skills.

Check Your *Interpretation Against* Traditional *Interpretations*

When we come up with an interpretation of a Scripture passage or a doctrinal conclusion, it's a good idea to test it against the wisdom of those who have gone before us. None of us is so brilliant or spiritually attuned that we cannot benefit from learning from others.

Exciting new interpretations of the Scriptures are always surfacing. But when it comes to understanding the Bible, new is not necessarily preferable. Accuracy is preferable. If we can avail ourselves of the lessons of church history and the accumulated wisdom of our predecessors in the faith, we can avoid many of the mistakes of the past and press on to accurate interpretation. Of course, tradition is not always right either. Commentaries, study tools, and theology books can assist us in our study, but ultimately the Bible itself is our guide to faith and living.

Our Theology Must Be Attuned with Reason

God communicates with us in a way that entails the use of reason. Therefore, our theology should always make good, logical sense. G. K. Chesterton has written that "theology is only thought applied to religion."[3] An intelligent approach to God's revelation is a theology that makes rational sense.

A theological belief must demonstrate three major criteria:

1. *Logical noncontradiction.* Something cannot be both true and false at the same time. The truth reflects the nature of He who is Truth and is therefore inherently logical.

2. *Empirical adequacy.* We must be able to support what we believe with adequate evidence.

3. *Existential viability.* We must be able to practice what we believe in our daily lives. A doctrine that has no effect on the way we live is questionable. Our beliefs should be affirmable without hypocrisy.

In other words, the Christian faith is rational but not rationalistic. "Rational" in that it makes sense. We should live our Christian lives with our rational faculties, our brains, fully functioning. At the same time, our faith is not "rationalistic," for mind alone cannot fully grasp all that God has done for us. We cannot reduce our faith to a logical statement. It is so much more.

Allow for Paradox and Mystery

In our humanness, we can never grasp the whole of truth. Like Job, we must silence and humble ourselves before the truth and mystery of God. Truth often comes to us in the form of paradox—two equally true statements that we cannot completely manage to synthesize. We might call this "truth in tension." The truth exists in two statements which seem contradictory. For example, we believe in both the absolute sovereignty of God and in the absolute human freedom to respond to God. Somehow, these two truths are held together in tension. If we ignore either side of the equation, we reduce the awesome mystery of the truth and have only a half-truth. We cannot grasp the full and complete truth because our human intelligence is simply not capable of the task.

Approach Theology with Humility

We must face the fact that we can never master the full truth. We would have to be God to fully know as God knows.

Scripture reveals what is necessary for our salvation and for living fully for Him, but our knowledge is not exhaustive. We have certain limitations in the face of the glorious truth. Frederick Buechner offers this description of theology:

> Theology is the study of God and His ways. For all we know, dung beetles may study man and his ways and call it humanology. If so, we would probably be more touched and amused than irritated. One hopes that God feels likewise.[4]

When we attempt to uncover the riches of God's revelation, we must do so with a spirit of humility and of prayerfulness. Evagrius Ponticus, a fourth-century-church father wrote, "The theologian is the one who prays; and if you pray truly, you are a theologian." Spiritual writer and historian Benedicta Ward, echoes this thought: "I would like to think that the theologian is the one who prays correctly, not the one who merely thinks correctly. Christianity, after all, is not only a way of thinking."[5]

We must keep our limitations in mind and beware of the danger of pride for the Christian thinker. As our children learn more of the meaning and content of the Christian life, we need to make sure they do not mistake knowing about God for knowing God. There is a pertinent illustration of this in Charles Dickens' novel *Hard Times*. A tyrannical school teacher asks a young girl to define a horse. When she falters in her answer, the arrogant teacher, Mr. Gradgrind, calls on his prize pupil, Bitzer.

> "Bitzer," said Thomas Gradgrind, "your definition of a horse."
>
> "Quadruped. Gramnivorous. Forty teeth, namely twenty-four grinders, four eye-teeth, and twelve incisive. Sheds coat in the spring; in marshy countries sheds hoofs too. Hoofs hard, but requiring to be shod with iron. Age known by marks in mouth." Thus (and much more) Bitzer.

"Now girl number twenty," said Mr. Gradgrind, "you know what a horse is."[6]

This reminds me of many theologians who simply pass on a group of facts about God and His ways. This, by itself, only leads to spiritual arrogance.

We must try to avoid what the German theologian Helmut Thielicke called "infatuation with theological concepts." There is, he says, the danger of vanity to those who engage in theological thinking.

> Truth seduces us very easily into a kind of joy of possession: I have comprehended this and that, learned it, understood it. Knowledge is power. I am therefore more than the other man who does not know this and that. I have greater possibilities and also greater temptations. Anyone who deals with truth—as we theologians certainly do—succumbs all too easily to the psychology of the possessor. But love is the opposite of the will to possess. It is self-giving. It boasteth not itself, but humbleth itself.[7]

The Goal of Theology: Knowing God More Intimately

The study of the things of God leads to a sense of wonder and awe, and ultimately, to a posture of worship. Thomas Aquinas, one of the greatest theologians of all time, wrote a multivolume study of theology called the *Summa Theologica*. It was his attempt to summarize the entire theological enterprise, covering every area of theological understanding. But before it was finished, he mysteriously abandoned the project with the statement that all he had written was "straw" compared to what he had seen in mystical contemplation. For Aquinas, personal relationship with God far surpassed even the grandest theological scheme.

Knowing the things of God will drive us to know Him more intimately. We must always ask ourselves, "How does this new insight affect my life? How does it help me draw closer to my Savior?"

Theology, properly understood, is never an attempt to encompass God with understanding, to confine Him by definition and systematization. Such is the stuff of idolatry. This way of doing theology creates God in our own image. Instead, theology should help us see ourselves realistically as we stand in relationship with God, revealing our shortcomings in light of this relationship and challenging us to follow hard after truth.

You will know if you really understand something when you try to explain it to your children. And do not assume that your children could not understand the wondrous truths that God is teaching you. They are capable of much understanding. C. S. Lewis said this about making belief understandable:

> You must translate every bit of your Theology into the vernacular. This is very troublesome and it means you can say very little in half an hour, but it is essential. It is also of the greatest service to your own thought. I have come to the conviction that if you cannot translate your thoughts into uneducated language, then your thoughts were confused.[8]

Your children can begin to think theologically at a very early age. And if the truths of Scripture become a part of their mental furniture when they are young, they will most likely grow into teens and adults who can engage their minds on any question, allowing the light of God's truth to illuminate even the most thorny issue.

So, we must make sure that our children are cultivating their moral imaginations with positive content.

Marks of the Christian Mind

We will close this chapter with a brief look at the ideal content of the Christian mind. These minimal characteristics differentiate the Christian vision from that of the average non-believer.

1. *The Christian mind has a supernatural orientation.* The Christian believes that true reality goes beyond what we can see, touch, and feel. In fact, the ultimate reality is a God who is infinite (eternally existent), personal (knowable in a relationship), transcendent (above and beyond the earthly realm), immanent (present and approachable in the earthly realm), sovereign (His ultimate will is what will be done), omniscient (all-knowing), and omnipotent (all-powerful).

2. *The Christian mind has a deep awareness of evil.*
The Christian understands that our present reality on earth is not as God intended it to be. Human beings are created in the image of God, but fallen and in need of redemption. Because of this, evil is not merely an appearance, but a reality.

3. *The Christian mind is marked by a belief in objective truth.* The Christian believes in absolute truth. We may not always easily grasp the absolute truth, but we know that absolutes flow forth from our God and Creator. God's world is ordered and logical. He has chosen to communicate His absolute truth through the person of Jesus Christ and through the Scriptures.

4. *The Christian mind is marked by the acceptance of authority.* The Christian accepts God as the ultimate basis for morality and His commands that show us how to live our lives. We accept that God has ordained legitimate authority in the family, the state, and the church, and that our ultimate authority is always God Himself.

5. *The Christian mind is marked by a concern for others as persons.* The Christian sees others not as objects to be used or manipulated, but as creations of God worthy of respect and honor. Love for God and for others is the great commandment by which we live.

6. *The Christian mind is characterized by the belief that history has a purpose and a goal.* The Christian believes that life is not

just the result of chance and happenstance, but that God has a plan for the human race which is even now being brought to fruition. God entered human history in the person of His Son to redeem mankind and reconcile us to God. Our ultimate future will be to spend eternity with our loving Father in heaven.

Following are two lists of books which will help you as you develop a Christian worldview and explore the world of theology:

Books for Developing a Christian Mind

Harry Blamires, *The Christian Mind*

G. K. Chesterton, *Orthodoxy*; *The Everlasting Man*

Peter Kreeft, *Christianity for Modern Pagans*

Peter Kreeft and Ronald K. Tacelli, *Handbook of Christian Apologetics*

C. S. Lewis, *Mere Christianity*; *The Problem of Pain*

J. I. Packer, *Knowing God*

James Sire, *The Universe Next Door*

Books for the Budding Theologian

Donald Bloesch, *Essentials of Evangelical Theology* (2 volumes)

John Jefferson Davis, *Handbook of Basic Bible Texts*

Walter A. Elwell, *Evangelical Dictionary of Theology*

Millard J. Erickson, *Christian Theology*

H. Wayne House, *Charts of Christian Theology and Doctrine*

Helmut Thielicke, *A Little Exercise for Young Theologians*

He who cannot draw on three thousand years is living hand to mouth.

—Johann von Goethe

• • •

7

In Praise of Tradition

Discovering Our
Christian Heritage

*W*hen Sharon entered college, she was a bright and enthusiastic Christian. Four years later, her faith was more timid and less self-assured. Though she still clung to the emotional comforts of her faith, she gave up trying to integrate her faith with her intellectual pursuits. In the high-flown world of academia, her belief system seemed irrelevant and old-fashioned. Her evangelical commitment was, her professors told her, just one of many options in terms of intellectual frameworks. What Sharon had failed to understand before she entered college is that the Christian faith is not just a unique modern way of looking at life, but the single most powerful influence in the construction of western civilization. Her professors failed to point out the vital impact of a personal faith on innumerable artists, writers, and thinkers; that Christianity is not just a conservative fad, but a richly textured way of looking at life and of understanding our human existence. Sharon, like many Christian young people, had become intellectually embarrassed of her faith, but this embarrassment arose primarily because she lacked awareness of just how rich and diverse the Christian tradition really is. An awareness of our heritage as believers gives us a sense of confidence and pride in the face of a secularism which dismisses our faith as an empty, passing fad.

The growth of the moral imagination is not nourished by a constant diet of the new, but is enriched as we partake of the rich feast of the past. This goes against the grain of modern thinking. Tradition has a bad name in our society, and often in evangelical circles as well. When many people think of tradition, they think of a mindless following of old and antiquated ways. It is seen as an exterminator of spontaneity, as a shallow and lifeless substitution of yesterday's belief for today's practice. Yet, the Bible stresses the importance of handing down the riches of our faith. Part of our privilege as parents and educators is to teach our children to appreciate our Christian heritage, and to drink deeply at the wells of tradition.

In the Old Testament we see the importance of faith as a tradition, a heritage passed down from generation to generation. In the sixth chapter of the book of Deuteronomy we find that when Moses was given commandments for the people of God, parents were instructed to teach these commandments to their children and to pass them on to subsequent generations. And it was not only the commandments themselves that were to be taught, but the very history of God's dealings with His people.

There is a false perception that Jesus condemned tradition. Some point to passages like Mark 7:8,9 or Matthew 15:3 to demonstrate the supposed negative attitude Jesus held toward tradition. But a careful reading of these passages will clarify that it is not tradition itself that He condemned; only false and shallow tradition. Jesus condemned the kind of tradition that exalts itself above the commands of God and replaces religion of the heart with empty and lifeless formulas. This kind of tradition rests safely in the past without due appreciation for what God is doing in the present or will do in the future. It is a tradition which idolizes the past, but fails to see that the past is valuable to us primarily because it teaches us to live in the present.

Many fail to comprehend the difference between tradition and traditionalism. Jaroslav Pelikan differentiates between the two: Tradition is "the living faith of the dead," which can still affect us in positive ways, nurturing and challenging us, and traditionalism is "the dead faith of the living," which holds onto the outward rituals and rhetoric of belief but does not burn with an inner passion for God.

Living Tradition

Ultimately, tradition in the church is the ongoing living influence of the Holy Spirit. And the Holy Spirit is the spirit which makes all things new. Pascal wrote in one of his letters:

> The truths of Christianity are certainly new things, but they must be renewed continually . . . the things of the world, however new they be, grow old as they endure; whereas the new spirit continues to renew itself increasingly as it endures.

Because God is alive and His spirit is alive, the truth renews itself on a continual basis. But at the same time the truth is ever the same; it does not change. We do not look for new truth, but for the truth to constantly make itself heard anew. Simone Weil wrote that "to be always relevant, you have to say things which are eternal."

Tradition tells us that we need to stay attentive to the past and to what we can learn from it. According to G. K. Chesterton, tradition is the "democracy of the dead," the important task of learning from the wisdom of those who have gone before us:

> Tradition may be defined as an extension of the franchise. Tradition means giving votes to the most obscure of all classes, our ancestors. It is the democracy of the dead. Tradition refuses to submit to the small and arrogant oligarchy of those who merely happen to be walking about.[1]

Some argue that we do not need to listen to the voice of the past, that we only need to hear God in the present. Such a negative attitude toward tradition may be, at its root, a spiritual problem. It could indicate an overwhelming and arrogant pride in ourselves and our resources. I can remember, as a young Christian, being counseled against reading Bible commentaries and works of theology because all I really needed was the Bible itself. All that I needed to know could be clearly drawn from its pages. This idea troubled me until I realized the hidden arrogance of believing that I did not need the insights and revelations of those who had preceded me. To suggest that I would be harmed by the insights of brilliant and godly men and women of the past and present is a folly that is truly dangerous. Are we not the body of Christ? Is not the body of Christ extended over time as well as space? Do we not need each other? Are our ancestors in the faith of no importance today?

Indeed, all of our present achievements and insights are based upon ideas and discoveries which preceded them. We progress by listening to the past, by asking questions of it, sometimes by arguing with it. In his seminal essay *Tradition and Individual Talent*, T. S. Eliot has expressed well the concept of the correct use of the past:

> If the only form of tradition, of handing down, consisted in following the ways of the immediate generation before us in a blind or timid adherence to its successes, "tradition" should positively be discouraged. We have seen many such simple currents soon lost in the sand; and novelty is better than repetition. Tradition is a matter of much wider significance. It cannot be inherited, and if you want it you must obtain it by great labor.[2]

As Eliot points out, tradition is not the same as conformity. In considering the importance of tradition, we are not talking about a thoughtless following of past ways and ideas. Instead, what we must understand is that our contemporary work is part of a succession from the past, and that we function best in the present when we take the past into account. We do not need to reinvent the wheel in each generation. Can you imagine how slowly science would progress if each and every scientist had to go back to the beginning and rediscover the basic laws of science? Instead, scientists build on the work of those who have gone before them. So do we in every area of our lives every day.

Bernardus of Silvestris, a twelfth-century monk, wrote regarding the successes of his own day: "We see farther because we stand on the shoulders of giants." So it is for us. As believers we stand on the shoulders of the likes of Augustine, Aquinas, Luther, Calvin, and Jonathan Edwards. We build on their insights and use their perspectives to critique our own time. Sometimes it is difficult for us to see our own cultural attitudes and ideas clearly and objectively, because they are so much a part of us. Like the air around us, we cannot see them clearly because we are surrounded by them and they tend to become invisible. But from the vantage point of a former time and place, gained through attentive reading of the classics of our tradition, we can see how time-bound and ungodly some of our own cherished prejudices really are. "Someone has said: 'The dead writers are remote from us because we know so much more than they did.' Precisely," writes T. S. Eliot, "and they are that which we know."[3]

An attitude that is widespread in our culture is that our present time is so progressive we no longer have need of our "barbaric" past. Yes, our progress is easy to see in today's realm of technology and machinery. I have seen in my own lifetime rapid changes and transformations in all kinds of technology. What was once unthinkable is now almost humdrum. But unfortunately, the concept of constant progress which leaves the past behind has carried over into the realm of human thought and culture. That which is more recent is conceived of as more enlightened than what preceded it. C. S. Lewis labels this kind of thinking "chronological snobbery." Lewis writes in his autobiography about how his friend Owen Barfield questioned his youthful trust in the merely contemporary and how he was cured of this attitude:

> Barfield... made short work of what I have called my "chronological snobbery," the uncritical acceptance of the intellectual climate common to our age and the assumption that whatever has gone out of date is on that account discredited. You must find out why it went out of date; was it ever refuted (and if so by whom, where and how conclusively) or did it merely die away as fashions do? If the latter, this tells us nothing about its truth or falsehood. From seeing this one passes to the realization that our age is also a "period," and certainly has, like all periods, its own characteristic illusions. They are likeliest to lurk in those widespread assumptions which are so ingrained in the age that no one dares to attack or feels it necessary to defend them.[4]

When we treat the thinking of the past as irrelevant, we cut ourselves off from its riches. And we lose the opportunity to use the past as a source by which we can critique our own age.

Above all, tradition frees us from the siren-song of relevancy. All the voices around us are crying out the importance of making education "relevant." Unfortunately, what this often means is that we must make ourselves slaves of the contemporary, following the pied piper of the latest trend or fad. We use our perceived freedom from the constraints of the past to follow blindly the whims of the moment. We busily try to catch the next wave of innovation. But as Dean Inge wrote, "He who is married to the spirit of the age will soon find himself a widower." While the "relevant" is ever shifting and changing, the truths embedded in tradition remain constant.

Tradition is not only constant, but is a fountainhead of creativity. Paradoxically, the work of artists and thinkers who immersed themselves in the traditions of the past are among the most creative. Pablo Picasso, T. S. Eliot, and James Joyce all made striking innovations in their fields. All of them were patient students of the traditions out of which their art arose.

The past is a priceless treasure. We need to recapture a sense of our place in the unfolding of God's plan for the ages, and an appreciation for the "communion of saints," the contribution of believers throughout time. Thomas Oden, a theologian who spent much of his early theological career focused on the latest cultural and theological whims, has become increasingly committed to the importance of the writings of the early church. "Once hesitant to trust anyone over 30," he writes, "now I hesitate to trust anyone under 300." Oden bemoans the lack of historical perspective he sees in the modern church,

> [We] now need to recover a sense of the active work of the Spirit in history, through living communities. Our modern individualism too easily tempts us to take our Bible and remove ourselves from the wider believing community. We end up with a Bible and a radio, but no church.[5]

And so I put forth the challenge to reacquaint yourself with the riches of the Christian tradition. Read the great books of the Christian tradition, study them in groups, pass them around in churches, teach their ideas to your children. I have spent a number of years developing a list of books in the Christian tradition which could be considered truly "great books." It is not definitive, but it might be helpful. You will find an abbreviated form of this list at the end of this chapter.

Why Read the Christian Classics?

In the church today there is an abysmal lack of awareness both of the historical rootedness and the creative richness of our faith. Reading the Christian classics will heighten our awareness of these things with a number of positive results.

First, reading about Christians in previous cultures will help us to appreciate the diversity within the body of Christ, both currently and over time. Our differences may be real, but as we grow in awareness of the variety of ideas and the possible ways of expressing them within the Christian tradition, we will begin to see how few there are in history who agree with us on every point. This will cause us to focus less on the need to always be right and more on what C. S. Lewis called "mere Christianity," the handful of essential ideas that distinguish Christianity from other faiths and ideologies. Several common themes run throughout the great Christian writings, and we can learn even from those with whom we have violent disagreements. For example, while Calvinists and Arminians may disagree about providence, free will, and human freedom, Calvinists can learn to appreciate the penetrating insights of John Wesley; and Arminians, the rich thought of John Calvin. In so doing, we might find ourselves striking new positions of balance and tolerance. Also, we can more clearly understand our own positions when we see them set up against the positions of others as articulated by our "adversaries" themselves.

Second, the classics demonstrate the depth and profundity of our tradition. Many accuse orthodox Christianity of being anticultural. A tradition which can boast of the likes of Bach, Dostoevski, Rembrandt, Kierkegaard, Roualt, Flannery O'Connor, Donne, Handel, Dante, and Pascal cannot fairly be dismissed as narrow, sterile, and lacking in creative thrust. As the contemporary songwriter/performer T-Bone Burnett has written:

> I was asked, "Do you think Christianity is a fad?"
> "A fad," I wondered.
> And I thought about C. S. Lewis and G. K. Chesterton
> And T. S. Eliot.
> And I thought about Tolstoy and Dostoevski.
> And Reubens and van Gogh and Rembrandt.
> And Handel and Haydn and Bach.
> And Luther.

And Pascal.
And Dante Alighieri.
And à Kempis and Augustine.
And Paul of Tarsus and Simon Peter.
"It's been going on for years," I thought.
"Back to about one."

In a world whose memory
Goes back to about 1963,
A world cut off from the past,
It is important to discover our history.
Because we are all leaves on a tree.[6]

We can take pride in our heritage. Some of the finest artistic and creative achievements of all time are born out of the Christian gospel.

Third, the classics can help us understand how perennial the great questions of our faith are. Who is God? What is His role in human existence? What is mankind? What is our essential nature? What does the future hold? These books provide ever-new insights into these great questions. We can read these books again and again as they always have something new to say to us and provide resources for the continued discussion of these issues. And, because they oftentimes disagree with one another, we learn to read dialectically, with an open and questioning mind. These authors share in a dialogue which has occurred over the ages, concerning the nature of God and man, the purpose of human life, and the methods and beliefs which further that purpose. Mortimer Adler and Robert Hutchins have called it the "great conversation." On this side of eternity, there is much we do not understand. This dialogue, these arguments, this conversation, helps us draw closer to the truth. In some other cases, whether or not the author belongs in the Christian tradition will be a matter for debate. But even the heretics can teach us in that they will cause us to look more closely at the questions. Liberal and conservative, Protestant and Catholic and Eastern Orthodox—they are all worth reading.

Fourth, reading in the classics will give us a perspective that is broader than the merely contemporary. We are often prone to faddishness, concerned about the ephemeral and transient rather than the weighty and eternal. We debate issues like biblical prophecy, attempting to discern the signs of the last days and to "pin the tail on the Antichrist." I worked nearly ten years in a Christian bookstore, and saw how theological fads come and go with alarming rapidity. Yesterday's burning issue becomes forgotten tomorrow, as we dizzily chase yet another trend. Grounding ourselves in the great traditions of the church will keep us properly skeptical of the "latest thinking" and focused on the the critical essentials of the Christian faith.

Fifth, these works can help us understand that Christianity is not just an abstract set of beliefs, but a vision of reality. Sometimes we get so wrapped up in doctrine we forget that the Christian faith is a comprehensive way of viewing the world, what Edith Schaeffer called "a way of seeing." Fine art, poetry, and fiction, in particular, are a rich part of our heritage in the way they provide us with a creative vision of the world and our place in it. They demonstrate how the Christian sees the world in a different light than the non-believer. And this vision, as these classic works will demonstrate, is one marked by a realism about human limitations, coupled with profound hope, and glorious promise.

Sixth, the classics can teach us about the mistakes and triumphs of those who have gone before us. These books should not be thought of as an infallible source of wisdom but a record of much wisdom and insight. They are also a record of false starts, wrong conclusions, human frailty, and stubbornness. These writers are fallen individuals with faulty preconceptions and self-deceptions. But even these mistakes can enlighten us as sometimes we can only fully discern the truth in juxtaposition with error.

So, when we set about educating our children, it's important to introduce them as soon as possible to the richness of our Christian tradition. Reading and discussing the great books, listening to the great music, contemplating the great artistic achievements will help us to broaden their education, invigorate their imaginations, challenge their thinking, and train their aesthetic sense. The Christian classics are their heritage from the past that will enrich them their entire lives long.

Some Important Books in the Christian Tradition

This list makes no claim to be exhaustive, but focuses on those books and thinkers who have had a great impact on the church as a whole.

You may not agree with everything in every book on this list. The authors of these books even have serious disagreements with each other. And some on this list barely squeak into the Christian tradition because of the heterodoxy of some of their ideas (William Blake, for example). Still, their role in helping to shape our tradition makes them worthy of our attention.

Few of these books are readily understandable by younger readers. This list is more oriented to the parent, who can read and pass down information and then, as the child grows, introduce these important works.

I have marked a few of the books with asterisks. These are the ones I believe every Christian should read. They are the cream of a very impressive crop.

THE ANCIENT WORLD

**The Bible (of course!)

The Apostolic Fathers

Athanasius, *On the Incarnation*

The Desert Fathers (Thomas Merton has made a fine collection of their writings under the title *The Wisdom of the Desert*).

Augustine,
  ** *Confessions*
  The City of God

St. Benedict, *The Rule of St. Benedict*

THE MIDDLE AGES

Anselm of Canterbury, *Monoloium and Proslogium*

Bernard of Clairvaux, *On the Love of God*

Peter Abelard, *Letters of Abelard and Heloise*

Francis of Assisi, *Little Flowers of St. Francis*

Thomas Aquinas, *Summa Theologica*

Dante Alighieri,
  La Vita Nuova
  ** *The Divine Comedy*

The Cloud of Unknowing (author unknown)

Juliana of Norwich, *Revelations of Divine Love*

Geoffrey Chaucer, *The Canterbury Tales*

** Thomas à Kempis, *The Imitation of Christ*

THE EARLY MODERN PERIOD

Martin Luther,
  The Freedom of the Christian
  ** *Bondage of the Will*
  Table Talk

Ignatius of Loyola, *Spiritual Exercises*

John Calvin, *Institutes of the Christian Religion*

Teresa of Avila,
   **Interior Castle*
   The Way of Perfection

John of the Cross, *The Dark Night of the Soul*

**William Shakespeare, *Plays* (especially *Hamlet*,
   Macbeth, *King Lear*, *The Merchant of Venice*,
   Othello, *Romeo and Juliet*)

Lanelot Andrewes, *Private Devotions*

**Francis de Sales, *Introduction to the Devout Life*

John Donne, *Poems and selected sermons*

George Herbert, *Poems*

John Milton, *Paradise Lost*

**Brother Lawrence, *The Practice of the Presence of God*

**Blaise Pascal, *Pensees*

George Fox, *Journal*

**John Bunyan, *The Pilgrim's Progress*

Phillip Jakob Spener, *Pia Desideria*

Thomas Traherne, *Centuries of Meditation*

Madame Jeanne Guyon,
   Experiencing the Depths of Jesus Christ

Francis Fenelon, *Christian Perfection*

Daniel Defoe, *Robinson Crusoe*

THE EIGHTEENTH CENTURY

Jonathan Swift, *Gulliver's Travels*

Jean Paul deCaussade, *Abandonment to Divine
   Providence*

William Law, *A Serious Call to the Devout and
   Holy Life*

Jonathan Edwards, *Treatise on Religious Affections*

John Wesley, *Journal*

William Blake, *Songs of Innocence and Experience*

NINETEENTH CENTURY

Friedrich Schleiermacher, *On Religion*

Samuel Taylor Coleridge, *Poems*

Jane Austen,
  Pride and Prejudice
  Emma

Charles Finney, *Lectures on Revivals of Religion*

John Henry Newman, *Apologia Pro Vita Sua*

Robert Browning, *Poems*

Sören Kierkegaard,
  Fear and Trembling
  Sickness Unto Death
  The Attack Upon Christendom

Anthony Trollope,
  The Warden
  Barchester Towers

Fyodor Dostoevski,
  Crime and Punishment
  ***The Brothers Karamazov*

**George MacDonald,
  Fairy Tales
  ***At the Back of the North Wind*
  The Princess and the Goblin

Leo Tolstoy,
  War and Peace
  **Anna Karenina
  The Death of Ivan Ilyich

Hannah Whitall Smith, *The Christian's Secret to a Happy Life*

Charles Spurgeon, *Sermons*

**Gerard Manley Hopkins, *Poems*

Oswald Chambers, *My Utmost for His Highest*

Therese of Lisieux, *The Story of a Soul*

Author unknown, *The Way of the Pilgrim*

THE TWENTIETH CENTURY

**G. K. Chesterton,
Orthodoxy
The Everlasting Man
The Man Who Was Thursday

Evelyn Underhill, *Mysticism*

Jacques Maritain, *True Humanism*

Francois Mauriac,
Therese Desqueyroux
Vipers Tangle

Karl Barth,
The Word of God and the Word of Man
Church Dogmatics

Charles Williams, *Descent Into Hell*

Paul Tillich, *The Courage to Be*

**T. S. Eliot,
Poems (especially *Four Quartets*)
The Cocktail Party

Georges Bernanos, *Diary of a Country Priest*

Gabriel Marcel, *The Mystery of Being*

Boris Pasternak, *Doctor Zhivago*

J. R. R. Tolkien, *The Lord of the Rings*

Reinhold Niebuhr,
Moral Man and Immoral Society
The Nature and Destiny of Man

Thomas Kelly, *A Testament of Devotion*

Dorothy L. Sayers,
 The Man Born to Be King
 The Mind of the Maker
 The Whimsical Christian

H. Richard Niebuhr, *Christ and Culture*

**A. W. Tozer, *The Pursuit of God*

C. S. Lewis,
 ***Mere Christianity*
 ***The Screwtape Letters*
 ***The Chronicles of Narnia*
 The Abolition of Man
 Till We Have Faces
 Surprised by Joy

Ignazio Silone, *Bread and Wine*

Evelyn Waugh,
 A Handful of Dust
 Brideshead Revisited

Graham Greene,
 The Power and the Glory
 The Heart of the Matter
 The End of the Affair
 Monsignor Quixote

Dietrich Bonhoeffer,
 The Cost of Discipleship
 Letters and Papers from Prison

Helmut Thielicke,
 The Waiting Father
 Theological Ethics

Simone Weil, *Waiting for God*

Walker Percy,
 The Moviegoer
 Love in the Ruins
 The Second Coming

Thomas Merton,
  The Seven Storey Mountain
  Thoughts in Solitude
  New Seeds of Contemplation

Flannery O'Connor,
  Wise Blood
  Mystery and Manners
  A Good Man is Hard to Find
  Everything That Rises Must Converge

Martin Luther King, *Strength to Love*

Malcolm Muggeridge,
  Jesus Rediscovered
  The End of Christendom
  Something Beautiful for God

Francis Schaeffer,
  The God Who Is There
  How Should We Then Live?

SOME CONTEMPORARIES (candidates for greatness)

Jacques Ellul,
  The Presence of the Kingdom
  Prayer and Modern Man

Alexander Solzhenitsyn,
  One Day in the Life of Ivan Denisovich
  The First Circle
  Cancer Ward
  The Gulag Archipelago
  Nobel Lecture

Frederick Buechner,
  The Book of Bebb
  Telling the Truth
  Godric

Walter Wangerin,
  The Book of the Dun Cow
  Ragman and Other Cries of Faith

Shusaku Endo, *The Silence*

Henri Nouwen,
    The Way of the Heart
    Genesee Diary

Richard Foster,
    Celebration of Discipline
    Prayer

Dallas Willard, *The Spirit of the Disciplines*

Annie Dillard,
    A Pilgrim at Tinker Creek
    Teaching a Stone to Talk
    The Writing Life

Will Campbell, *Brother to a Dragonfly*

Charles Colson,
    Kingdoms in Conflict
    The Body

Sheldon Vanauken, *A Severe Mercy*

Peter Kreeft, *Heaven: the Heart's Deepest Longing*

If you would like to read further in the classics, I have created an annotated listing of these books and others from outside the Christian tradition which are worth knowing. The annotations will give you some idea of the significance, difficulty, and entertainment value of these books. This resource, *Great Books of the Christian Tradition*, will be available from Harvest House Publishers in late 1995.

All truth is God's truth.

—Francis Schaeffer

.   .   .

8

Spoiling the Egyptians

Extracting Truth from Secular Sources

hen I first saw a certain math textbook published by a Christian publisher, my immediate response was to chuckle. What struck me funny were the math equations that filled this elementary text. In the normal secular math book, the student counts apples, puppies, raindrops, etc. But in this text the child counted Bibles, crosses, and churches. The whole enterprise struck me as kind of silly. But, on further reflection, it began to bother me. Not because there was anything wrong with counting Bibles or disciples, but because this process implied that somehow these things were more "Christian" than the other items which filled the child's world. The implication was that there was a Christian math which was different, and possibly superior, to secular math.

But there is no such thing as "Christian math." Mathematics is the same whether you are a Christian or a non-Christian. Two plus two equals four whether it is four apples, four sports cars, or four Bibles. The idea that there is a specifically Christian form of math, science, history, or art is absurd. It is also poor theology. I believe there is a more biblical and theologically sound approach to learning, one that emphasizes the need to learn to read with discernment.

As modern Christians, we have created our own subculture. We have Christian music, Christian bookstores, Christian television, Christian schools, and just about anything else you might think of. There are some good things about this, but one of the dangers is that we can tend to devalue that which does not specifically wear the label "Christian." When we separate ourselves to this extent, we lose our impact upon the culture at large and rob ourselves of the insights we could draw from those whose faith is different from ours.

The Two Types of Revelation

There is a false form of spirituality which draws a sharp distinction between the earthly and heavenly spheres and dismisses the things of earth as unimportant. This is not biblical Christianity, but rather a form of Gnosticism or Neoplatonism. Biblical faith values the created order and believes that God is working out His purposes within the earthly sphere. When God became man in the person of Jesus Christ, He forever sanctified what it means to be human. And so the human, earthly sphere of existence is never to be dismissed or taken lightly. Let us not try to be more spiritual than God Himself is.

Theologians differentiate between two types of revelation, and it is here, perhaps, that the misunderstandings lie. The first is *general revelation* and is available to all people everywhere. The glories of nature, the innate moral law within us, and the logic of the created order are all sources which reveal something of God to us. These same sources are the basis for understanding God's created world. The second form of revelation is *special revelation*. Its primary focus is the revelation of God in the person of Jesus Christ, but it also includes the inspired record of God's dealings with His people, the Bible. Thomas Aquinas called these two forms of revelation "God's two books."

As believers, our priority is special revelation, especially when it instructs us about the things of God. Where general revelation is often vague and cloudy (note the plethora of confusion in man-made religions which are based on general revelation), the special revelation of Scripture is clear about the essential elements of man's redemption and relationship with God. So, in the area of theology and personal holiness, we are better off focusing our attention on special revelation as given us in the Scriptures.

When we turn to matters of science, history, and medicine, however, special revelation has some limitations. Though it does make some true statements about these areas, it does not speak exhaustively of them. And so we must turn to the data of general revelation to complete our knowledge. For example, the Bible tells us that God is the creator of the cosmos, but offers few details about how it was done. Likewise, the Bible says nothing about the intricacies of quantum physics, medical science, botany, or geology. This is not a shortcoming in the Bible; it's just that the dispensing of this kind of information is not its purpose. God has "written" another book to fulfill this purpose—general revelation. When the Bible speaks, we need to listen and respect its authority. But when it is silent, God expects us to use reason and creativity to experiment, inquire, and explore the book of nature. Because these two "books" have the same author, when they both speak on a topic, they will not contradict each other. If we think we see a contradiction, it is because we have misunderstood either Scripture or the facts of creation. Such contradictions are only apparent.

The Biblical Teaching on General Revelation

The Bible indicates that we can learn a great deal if we attend carefully to God's created world. Psalm 19 points to two different sources which can instruct us in the power and majesty of God: the book of nature (verses 1-6), and the book of the law (verses 7-14). Both Scripture and the created order speak to us of God's character:

> The heavens declare the glory of God; the skies proclaim the work of his hands. Day after day they pour forth speech; night after night they display knowledge. There is no speech or language where their voice is not heard. Their voice goes out into all the earth, their words to the ends of the world (Psalm 19:1-4).

When we train ourselves to attentiveness, having "ears to hear," nature speaks to us of the truth. Romans 1:18-32 offers us a similar acknowledgment of nature's revelation: "For since the creation of the world God's invisible qualities—his eternal power and divine nature—have been clearly seen, being understood from what has been made, so that men are without excuse" (Romans 1:20). Of course, as Paul points out, this knowledge is often ignored or perverted by sinful human beings. This is why we need the special revelation of God in Christ and the Word of God; general revelation is not enough to save us, only enough to make us realize our predicament.

We can see this worked out in Paul's life and ministry. Paul appealed in at least two instances to knowledge outside of special revelation. In Acts 14:15-17, Paul and Barnabas were preaching in Lystra. When the people of the city mistakenly thought Paul and Barnabas were gods and wanted to sacrifice to them, Paul rebuked them, assuring them that he and Barnabas were not gods. However, Paul pointed out that they had no excuse for ignorance of the living God for "He has not left himself without testimony" (14:17). Here Paul was speaking not to Jews, but to Greeks, and indicated that they could have had some knowledge of the true God even though they were not recipients of special revelation.

In Acts 17:22-31, Paul was preaching to Greeks again, this time in Athens. When he saw that they had constructed an altar to "the Unknown God," he used it as an opportunity to draw a connection between what they already knew and the good news of the gospel. The God they did not know was the God Paul revealed to them. In building his case, Paul did something interesting—in verse 28, he quoted one of their own pagan poets as a familiar and accurate source of information. Paul was not afraid to use secular sources when those sources spoke the truth. The reason Paul could do this was because he was committed to all truth as God's truth. There is not a "Christian truth" which is separate from "non-Christian" truth.

General Revelation in the Christian Tradition

Because all truth is God's truth, the early Christian theologian Justin Martyr could write, "Whatever has been well said anywhere or by anyone belongs to us Christians" (*Apology* II, 13). This is an attitude not of arrogance, but of gratitude. Gratitude for all the truth of God and His creation; the truths of science, art, sociology, psychology, as well as the truth of faith. Great thinkers throughout Christian history have pointed out that all knowledge is the province of the believer, that we have nothing to fear and everything to gain from the pursuit of truth wherever we find it. We must, as Augustine writes, mine the riches from the secular culture:

> All branches of human learning have not only false and superstitious fancies . . . but they contain also liberal instruction which is better adapted to the use of truth, and some most excellent precepts of morality; and some truths in regard even to the worship of the one God are found among them. Now these are, so to speak, their gold and silver, which they did not create themselves, but dug out of the mines of God's providence which are everywhere scattered abroad.[1]

John Calvin held to a similar philosophy:

> Whenever, therefore, we meet with heathen writers, let us learn from that light of truth which is admirably

displayed in their works, that the human mind, fallen as it is, and corrupted from its integrity, is yet invested and adorned by God with excellent talents. If we believe that the Spirit of God is the only fountain of truth, we shall neither reject nor despise the truth itself, wherever it shall appear, unless we wish to insult the Spirit of God.[2]

We can rejoice in what we can learn from secular sources, but possibly even more important is our responsibility to bring God's redemptive work to bear on every area of knowledge. As Francis Schaeffer wrote:

We must consciously reject the Platonic element which has been added to Christianity. God made the whole man; the whole man is redeemed in Christ. And after we are Christians, the Lordship of Christ covers the whole man. That includes his so-called spiritual things and his intellectual, creative and cultural things; it includes his law, his sociology, and psychology; it includes every single part and portion of a man and his being.[3]

Can we humbly admit that, as Christians, we do not have a corner on the truth? Staying open to learn, even from those with whom we violently disagree, is more than charity and courtesy; it is wisdom.

Learning from Nonbelievers

The title of this chapter, "Spoiling the Egyptians," captures the experience of the modern Christian. As the Israelites rose from bondage in Egypt, so the Christian must rise from the limitations of the modern secular worldview. We have found the promise of freedom just as they did. In our case, it is freedom from the stifling effects of a view of the world that ignores the basic truths of God's existence, power, and love, and also of human sinfulness and self-deception. To grasp these truths truly changes the way we think and live. The Israelites did not leave Egypt without "spoiling" their captors.

They brought with them anything they could find which was valuable and worthy. So too, we must make use of all of the truths we can find in so-called "secular" thinking. (Of course, there really is no such thing There are only true and false ways of thinking. The true ways of thinking are those rooted in correct interpretations of one or both of God's two forms of revelation.) And so we can learn much from our "Egyptian" captors!

One reason we can learn so much from unbelievers is that Christian values have influenced our culture so deeply that even unbelievers hold to remnants of truth. Most of our culture's moral foundations, institutions, and attitudes are based on Christian principles. This situation may be changing. Our worldview is becoming less and less acceptable and the common ground is shrinking. But still, though the last couple of centuries may have distorted the truth, the Christian influence in our culture is far from extinguished.

Another reason we can learn from unbelievers is that Christianity is about truth and reality. Unbelievers and believers alike share the same reality. When authors write about reality, they cannot escape the deep truths about human nature and man's sinfulness. Many great novelists and philosophers, without using the phraseology, write about man's fallenness.

Each age asks different questions about human identity, meaning, and purpose, and we must have enough compassion for our world to learn these questions. The best of our modern novelists are articulating them and giving us a window into the mental, emotional, and spiritual struggles of our time. As we read these novelists, we gain understanding of how our contemporaries think, and so we are better equipped to make the good news of the gospel clear to them. They may ask questions to which they have no answers, and so we can point them to the answers resident in the purposes of God.

We must also remember that we have opponents who are active in the battle for men's hearts and minds, who purport to give answers to the basic human questions that are patently false. If we want to counteract their misleading teachings, we need to listen closely to what they are saying and then use both Scripture and human reason to address their error.

Whenever we become arrogant, thinking we have a corner on the truth, we must remember that God used the Assyrians as a tool to correct Israel. These idol worshipers were God's instrument to shape His people. In the same way, if we are open today, we will hear Him use modern thinkers to correct the church. Though most of us would have serious disagreements with the likes of Marx, Sartre, and Nietzsche, the church would do well to hear their words of correction on the subjects of authenticity, pharisaism, justice, and our current ineffectuality. Gregory, an early Church Father, suggested we use secular culture as the Israelites did when they went to the Philistines to have their knives sharpened. We must learn to read dialectically, engaging in a conversation with the authors, questioning and challenging, as well as learning from them.

The best of our western culture is a storehouse for the best sub-Christian values. While these values don't tell the whole story, they are nonetheless important in our society. These are values of the soul, not the spirit. They will not bring redemption, but then again, God created the soul as well as the spirit.

Our phrase "giving the devil his due," according to the *Oxford English Dictionary*, means "to do justice even to a person of admittedly bad character or repute (or one disliked by the speaker)." We need humility, fairness, and objectivity to admit the truth, no matter the source.

If we want to navigate through the complexity and confusion of modern thought, we must have a thorough understanding of the Christian worldview. We must be intimately acquainted with the Scriptures if we are to withstand the onslaught of false teaching that comes to us along with the good insights. Obviously, this is a hard and demanding call—

to know the riches of Scripture and our Christian tradition while at the same time learning about our culture and its ideas. But it is a call to Christian scholarship. If Christian parents can capture this vision, they can raise children who will make a mark for Christ on our culture by their personal integrity, creativity, and razor-sharp intelligence. This is a force which can truly transform our world.

I tell you the truth, unless you change and become like little children, you will never enter the kingdom of heaven.

—Matthew 18:2

Not in entire forgetfulness,
And not in utter nakedness
But trailing clouds of glory do we come
From God who is our home:
Heaven lies about us in our infancy!

—William Wordsworth

•　　•　　•

9

The Spiritual Lives of Children

Making God Real in Their Hearts

*M*any believe, myself included, that children have an innate sense of God's reality. This is a precious thing, and should not be ignored, demeaned, or underestimated, but instead fostered, gently nourished, and allowed to grow—in its own time. We must resist the tendency to rush, crowd, or push our children, but rather gently guide and encourage them, removing hindrances and setting an example by our own spirituality. As a host introduces his guests to one another, so must we introduce Jesus Christ to our kids.

We can harm our children by forcing participation in religious rituals, using spiritual practices as a punishment, or holding unrealistic expectations about their spiritual maturity. Instead, we should function as midwives for the birth of spirituality in our children. A midwife does not drag the baby from the mother's womb but assists the mother in her own work of giving birth. So too, we must gently guide and lead, only interfering when the health of the spiritual baby is in jeopardy. Kids, like all of us, stick with decisions that are their own better than they do with those that are forced upon them.

Of course, this does not mean waiting for spiritual growth to magically occur. We can do specific things to help our children to maturity. I see three definite areas in which we can assist and participate in the spiritual growth of our children. These areas are: 1) helping them understand the presence of God in their lives; 2) introducing them to Bible reading; and 3) teaching them to pray.

The Sense of God's Presence

The poets have long told us that children have a special realization of the reality of God and a special awareness of His presence. Not bogged down by the skepticisms and dulled senses of adulthood, children see the world more as it really is. Later, as they mature, this sensitivity to God's presence is crowded out by the cares of the world. But in the meantime, the way in which a child relates to his or her heavenly Father is both tender and real. Walter Wangerin captures the unspoken wonder of God's presence in the life of the child:

> Who can say when, in any child, the dance with God begins? No one. Not even the child can later look back and remember the beginning of it, because it is as natural an experience (as early and as universally received) as the child's relationship with the sun or with his bedroom. And the beginning, specifically, cannot be remembered because in the beginning there are no words for it. The language to name, contain, and to explain the experience comes afterward. The dance, then, the relationship with God, faithing, begins in a mist. . . . [F]aithing, we may say, is not unique to a few people: it is at least initiated in all. It is a universal human experience. We all have danced one round with God. But we danced it in the mists.[1]

Children have this innate sense, but many of them fail to grow in it and eventually lose it because no one is there to help them understand it. As parents we have the awesome privilege of helping our children in their understanding of the love of God that surrounds and envelops them. We get to introduce them to their heavenly Father to whom they may open up their hearts. Children seem confident of the reality of God even at the earliest age. We need to nurture this sensitivity and explain its meaning to them.

Children do better with concrete images than with barren abstractions. For example, the image of "God's watchful eye" is one which children can easily grasp. It helps them make sense of the feeling of God's presence in their lives. The image of God's watchful eye can both challenge and comfort them. First, it challenges them when they realize that God sees everything they do. Unlike parents, who are often easy to fool, God is aware of all of our actions. He sees all of our activities and understands all of our motivations. This is, of course, a prod toward good behavior. Children need to understand that they cannot hide their bad behaviors, that Someone always sees and knows. This reinforces in children the knowledge of their own shortcomings, their sin. Children must learn that they cannot simply follow their desires without any consequences. One very real consequence of bad behavior is that it is painful to the God who loves them so. Despite what Freud thought, a proper sense of guilt is a good thing! Certainly, this can get out of hand; self-loathing is never healthy. But a sense of sin is an important aspect of moral growth.

The second element in the image of God's watchful eye keeps this sense of sin in balance: the comfort of walking through our lives with the love of God. To know that God is watching is also to know that God is watching over. We can help children to understand that God looks on us with eyes of love, with affection and concern. He is quick to forgive us our wrongdoings and renew our hearts. To teach guilt without teaching forgiveness is to do more harm than good. If children fail to understand the forgiving love of God, they will only harden their hearts in despair at their inability to live up to His standards. But when they understand God's forgiveness, that He looks past their sins, it helps them learn to look past the sins of others.

When our children know that God is watching over them, they are comforted in times of hurt and pain. They learn that they do not walk alone, that an invisible presence is with them in their struggles, that Jesus walks with them in their pain. When they are disappointed by the unfulfilled promises of an adult, when they are chosen last for the baseball team, when others mock them for their physical imperfections or ridicule their limitations of understanding, Jesus is with them. I remember the overpowering fear of going to a new school when my parents moved to a new city. I had fought long and hard for acceptance in my previous school, and now I would have to face that painful ordeal all over again. I was terrified. But I had memorized Psalm 23, and as I embarked on my first day at my new school, the words of this psalm, which promised God's presence with me, gave me strength and confidence:

> The Lord is my shepherd, I shall not be in want.
> He makes me lie down in green pastures,
> He leads me beside quiet waters,
> He restores my soul.
> He guides me in the paths of righteousness for his name's sake.
> Even though I walk through the valley of the shadow of death,
> I will fear no evil, for you are with me;
> Your rod and your staff, they comfort me.
> You prepare a table before me in the presence of my enemies.
> You anoint my head with oil; my cup overflows.
> Surely goodness and love will follow me all the days of my life,
> And I will dwell in the house of the Lord forever.

To know God in His love and righteousness is to be able to walk in moral uprightness. Without the awareness of a loving

God watching over us, we have little hope of living a life of moral purity.

Reading the Bible

Over the years I have memorized many passages of Scripture that have been lifelines to me in times of struggle and difficulty. We do our children a great service when we instill in them a love for the Scriptures.

As soon as they are old enough, give them short passages of Scripture to memorize. Some might argue that this is just rote memorization, but I have seen too many times in my own life, and that of others, how a passage of Scripture, long ago memorized, will rise to the surface of my mind at the exact time I need it most. To help our children memorize Scripture is to equip them with tools they can use in their journey through life. Sure, you can use a shoe to drive a nail or your fingers to turn a screw, but when you have the proper tools it is a much more effective undertaking. Scripture is a tool that helps us face and defeat the temptations of the enemy, that gives us assurance in times of doubt and despair, and helps us give guidance to those who call on us for advice. You will not always have a Bible in hand for such circumstances, but when you memorize Scripture, you will always carry the Word of God with you in your heart. As with everything else in the spiritual life, try not to make memorization a chore for your kids. One thing that works well is to offer some sort of prize or payment for every verse learned. This provides motivation and makes the process more fun. And as they grow they will eventually see that knowing Scripture is a reward in itself.

If you have very young kids, a children's story Bible is an important investment. Long before they can understand the deeper meanings of the Christian gospel, they can thrill to the excitement of the stories in the Bible. Children are natural pragmatists. They don't want to just hear about how things work, they want to see how things work. The stories of the Bible reveal God's work in the lives of people in the past. The stories of young people like themselves (David, Samuel) give them a picture of how they can live lives that are pleasing to God. Read these stories to them regularly and discuss the implications in their lives.

When your children are a bit older, give them a real Bible—one that is their very own. Even before they can actually read it, they can pack it around with them and take it to church, thereby establishing its importance in their lives. There is a delightful smile that breaks out on the faces of most children when they are presented with their first Bible. So make sure it is one they can take pride in, not a worn-out hand-me-down. You need not spend a lot of money—a small pocket-sized New Testament is just the right size for small hands and is easy on the pocketbook. If your Christian bookstore offers the service, have the child's name imprinted on the front cover. This gives a special sense of ownership and seems to earn the Bible special treatment. Instead of getting the usual "rough treatment" kids often give to their possessions, it will be cherished and taken care of. And it will be used. My youngest, when she received her first Bible at about age 3½, always waited for me to find the passage being read in church so that she could "follow along." Of course, she could not read the words, but her eyes scanned the page with great solemnity. She soon got the idea that this was a special book—one we could turn to for guidance, instruction, and comfort.

If children can learn to love the Word of God at an early age, it can begin a lifetime of reading the Scriptures. Just a couple of nights ago, long after bedtime had come and gone, I heard a suspicious rustling upstairs in my nine-year-old's bedroom. *Aha!* I thought. *I'll catch her in the act of playing with her toys instead of sleeping as she is supposed to.* I crept up the stairs, peered around the corner of her doorway, and caught her—lying in bed reading her Bible. *Oh well,* I thought, *this is one act of disobedience which I think I'll let pass.* I crept slowly back down the stairs.

Learning to Pray: the Habit of Prayer

The pinnacle of our spiritual lives is found in prayer. Our times of communion with God are the most important way we grow spiritually. Prayer is an exercise of trust, of committing our desires and disappointments to God. Prayer is allowing God to speak in the quietness of our hearts—to challenge our habits of sin, to bring us comfort, and to help us to grow in our spiritual discernment and commitment. These are, of course, all things our children need as much as we do. We cannot (and should not) force or intimidate our children into praying. Instead we can provide an invitation and example to the life of prayer. Prayer is not an activity; it is a way of life.

When we are discussing prayer with our children, we need to emphasize that prayer comes out of relationship with God. Children need to understand that prayer is not a magic formula or a rote repetition, but that it is talking with God Himself. Instead of asking our children, "Have you prayed about this?" we can ask them, "Have you talked with Jesus about this?" Help them understand that God is Someone to whom they can talk freely, Someone who loves us and desires to be a part of our lives. Emphasize that prayer is primarily a conversation with God.

Demonstrate to your children that prayer is a good habit to develop. Set aside specific times when prayer is part of the family ritual; at breakfast, at dinner, at bedtime. When the habit of prayer is built into their lives, they will find it natural to turn to God in times of need and crisis.

Use bedtime as an opportunity to develop your children's spiritual life. As you tuck your kids in, ask them about their day and about how they feel. The daytime hours are often too busy and stressful for any significant communication to take place. At night, before you turn out the lights, sit down on the edge of their bed and show them your love by encouraging them to unburden themselves, to talk about their fears, their failures, their disappointments, their hurts, and their triumphs. Let them see your concern and love for them. And then, once they have opened their hearts, you can show them how to take their needs before their Father in heaven.

Many children are too intimidated to pray aloud. Usually this stems from feelings of inadequacy. They cannot find the words to express themselves, so they close up. One solution to this is written prayers—set prayers they can memorize and then say themselves. Young children do best with simple prayers and prayer formulas. Since they do not often have the vocabulary to articulate their feelings and desires, these prayers can help them find the words.

Such prayers are not complex or theologically rich, but they can help children learn to address God in simple trust. Simple prayers, especially those with a poetic rhyme, are easy for children to learn and remember. When they are young, the habit of praying is probably more important than the content of the prayers. So, if you would like some examples of simple prayers to teach your children, you might want to examine one of the books of poetic prayers Tasha Tudor has written—*First Prayers* or *First Graces*.

As your children mature, you can teach them the Lord's Prayer, found in Matthew 6:9-13—the prayer Jesus gave to His disciples in response to their request, "Lord, teach us to pray" (Luke 11:1).

> Our Father who art in heaven,
> Hallowed be Thy name.
> Thy kingdom come
> Thy will be done,
> On earth as it is in heaven.
> Give us this day our daily bread.
> And forgive us our debts,
> As we also have forgiven our debtors.
> And do not lead us into temptation,
> But deliver us from evil.
> For Thine is the kingdom, and the power, and the glory,
> forever. Amen (NASB).

It is easier for children to learn this prayer than to understand it. You will need to explain the phrases and concepts to your children. In fact, as a family, you could study it line-by-line, extracting the underlying teachings and expanding upon them. For in this prayer we acknowledge the awesomeness of God, our own sinfulness, our trust in God for daily provision, and our need for God's strength and guidance to see us through the temptations of our lives. Finally, it ends on a note of hope and faith.

The Scriptures contain many other prayers we can teach to our children and help them to make their own. For example, David's prayer that God would reveal and root out sinful patterns in his life:

> Search me, O God, and know my heart;
> test me and know my anxious thoughts.
> See if there be any offensive way in me,
> and lead me in the way everlasting (Psalm 139:23,24).

Or, also from the Psalms, the words I often pray just before I do any public speaking:

> May the words of my mouth and the meditation of my
> heart be pleasing in your sight, O Lord, my Rock and my
> Redeemer (Psalm 19:14).

You'll find many similar prayers in the Psalms, the Epistles, and in the book of Revelation. These simple prayers can provide us with the words to express our own and our children's deepest feelings to the Lord.

Very young children are not able to learn these prayers yet. But they can learn short prayer formulas to get them started and that they can then fill in with their own words. For example, the phrase "Thank You, God..." will get them started on a list of things they are thankful for. "I'm sorry, God..." can be followed with a confession of their sins. Even the very young have an awareness of their sinfulness, and this prayer can teach them to search their hearts and confess specific sins, not just content themselves with a vague "Lord, forgive all my sins." A phrase like "Please help me, Lord..."

teaches petitionary prayer. Children need to learn early in life the joy of answered prayer and how to still trust God when they don't get exactly what they prayed for. Finally, it is important for kids to see the needs of others and not just focus on themselves. A prayer like, "Lord, please help..." will encourage them to practice compassion and break out of the self-centeredness which is so natural to children.

Of course, the goal is that eventually your children will be less reliant on formulaic prayers and will learn to pray in their own words. Though simple written prayers have their place (I use them often myself), there is no substitute for the expressions, feeble though they often are, of our own hearts. When you listen in on the extemporaneous and spontaneous prayers of your children, you will gain quite a unique glimpse of what is in their hearts.

Praying Honestly and Reasonably

The natural prayers of most children have two common qualities—honesty and boldness. The first should be encouraged, the second controlled.

Honesty before God is something many adults lose as they mature in their faith. We often get too pious to tell God how we really feel and too ashamed of our sins to want to admit to them. But this is not the biblical pattern of prayer. David, in the Psalms, is forthright about his feelings and emotions:

My thoughts trouble me and I am distraught...
My heart is in anguish within me...
Fear and trembling have beset me;
Horror has overwhelmed me... (Psalm 55:2,4,5).

He complains, rails, and accuses God of unfairness:

Will the Lord reject forever?
Will He never show His favor again?
Has His unfailing love vanished forever?
Has His promise failed for all time?

Has God forgotten to be merciful?
Has He in anger withheld His compassion?
(Psalm 77:7-9).

David can speak this honestly because he knows the Fatherly love of God. God cannot change our attitudes until we admit to having them. So when we express ourselves honestly, trusting in God's love, the door is open for Him to transform our misconceptions and bad attitudes. God knows our hearts; we cannot hide our feelings from Him. Better to admit to them and give Him the opportunity to change us. And this attitude is simply more natural for children than for adults. Children are less prone to play games with God, trying to convince Him of their goodness. They tend to let it all hang out—an attitude which develops a real and abiding trust, a prerequisite to any meaningful and intimate relationship with Him.

The second common characteristic of children's prayers is their boldness—a willingness to ask anything and everything of Him. Now this is in many ways a good thing; we are instructed to "come boldly before the throne of grace." However, with children this can degenerate into a silliness which asks for the inappropriate or the impossible. Children's natural tendency toward magical thinking can lead them to view prayer as a magic trick to get what they want. They must see that the purpose of prayer is not to help us avoid pain or guarantee success; that God is not a vending machine, ready to supply all of our wants. So if our children do not temper this magic thinking, the result will most likely be disappointment, confusion, and the seeds of unbelief. Many adults have turned against God because as children they felt that He had disappointed them or let them down. We can help our children to frame reasonable requests, not criticizing their excessive boldness, but tempering it by helping them see that God desires more out of their lives than simply to make them happy. He is the companion who sees us through our pain, gives us strength and courage, and opens our eyes to help us see things from His perspective—an eternal one.

When it comes to our children's spiritual lives, we must see ourselves as what we are: not creators, but caretakers. Try as we might, we cannot develop spiritual depth in our children. We cannot create for them a depth of relationship with God. Our children are a garden and God has given us the privilege of watering, pruning, and fertilizing. Our occupation is to help them grow by providing the atmosphere, the tools, and the example. The growth is up to God.

PART THREE

The Christian Vision

There is nothing more fearful than imagination without taste.

—Johann von Goethe

· · ·

10

The Moral Imagination and Culture

Why Is Shakespeare Better Than Stephen King?

*I*n this third section, we will examine how we might use our leisure time to develop our moral imagination. Once the stress and hassle of the day is over, and we plop down in our favorite chair, what do we do with our time? And what kind of example do we set for our children who are watching how we use this time? Of course, an occasional "veg out" session is fine; we all need to rest our minds and spirits from time to time. But when spending all of our leisure time on frivolous and vacant pursuits becomes habitual, our true priorities are not what they should be.

Leisure time can be a time to partake of the refreshment of truly worthwhile art, to exercise our creative urges, to learn something new, to study the Scriptures, to expand our mind, heart, and spirit.

If we are to help our children learn to use their leisure time wisely, we must do two things:

1. We must set a good example. If we spend large amounts of time vacantly staring into the television set or reading books that could only be classified as "rubbish," we should not be surprised if our children do the same. But when we use our time wisely, pursuing activities that expand and enrich us, our children will follow our example.

2. We must teach our children to discern the difference between the truly worthwhile and that which is not. Like their parents, children have a tendency to gravitate toward that which gives immediate pleasure rather than that which demands more of us in terms of concentration and contemplation. The television show "Gilligan's Island" is much more accessible than the book *Treasure Island*, but it also offers a lot less in the way of insight, information, and true adventure. We must expose our children to the best our heritage has to offer and teach them to appreciate what is truly worthy of our attention. One of Shakespeare's plays may be more difficult to read and demand more concentration than a second-rate children's book, but the rewards of reading it are infinitely greater.

What we strive for is what one educational philosopher has called "enlightened cherishing." We must teach our children to experience life aesthetically, truly cherishing what life has to offer them, sensing the drama inherent in each moment and each day. Otherwise, they will grow up to live their lives like automatons, experiencing each day in the dull confines of their preconceived stereotypes.

Often, our emotional lives are boxed in by our inability or unwillingness to make subtle discriminations. Many of our problems in life are caused by oversimplifications, especially oversimplified emotional responses. Consider, for example, the way many young people tend to view love.

Real love, as we learn from the Scriptures and from the classics, is a complex thing. It involves sacrificial self-giving and is a sometimes arduous task. The emotion of love is easily confused and intermingled with other emotions like jealousy, fear, anger, elation, and joy.

Many people, however, do not view love in all its complexity. They think of love in terms of the clichés which come so quickly to us: "Love is blind," "love is a many splendoured thing," "falling in love." For these people, love is a magical, mystical, inexplicable thing that happens to a person. Is it any wonder that marriages fail so often in our culture when our perspective of love is based on such a stereotypical, over-simplified view? It requires cultivation to get beyond such dull-mindedness, and one way such cultivation is practiced is through developing our aesthetic sensibilities. When our aesthetic sensitivities are developed, we can make proper discriminations and examine our own lives more thoroughly.

The inability to judge the good from the bad, the significant from the insignificant is a sign of aesthetic insensitivity. It demonstrates a real poverty in our lives. Harry S. Broudy writes:

> Aesthetic insensitivity is a clue to our unhappiness with life. For inability to sense subtle significance makes our lives drab, routinized, and boring. It renders us vulnerable to drugs and other bizarre stimulations in search of proof that we are alive and not existential zeros. The need for such proof is a sign of desperation, what Soren Kierkegaard called existential despair.[1]

In the pages of this section you will learn how you can help your children value the right things, appreciate the true and the beautiful, and learn proper discrimination. You will also learn how the moral imagination can be impaired or enhanced by the cultural diet your children are exposed to. Hopefully, these chapters will challenge you to improve your own cultural diet as well.

I find television very educational. When it's
on I go into the other room and read a book.

—Groucho Marx

•　　•　　•

11

Television: The One-Eyed Bandit

Rethinking Our Reliance on Television

I was like most kids of my generation. I would stretch out for seemingly endless hours in front of the television set. I cannot say that I was a discerning viewer. I would watch just about anything, though I did have my favorites: "Gilligan's Island," "Wild Wild West," "The Brady Bunch," "Sanford and Son." For those of my generation, the very titles probably evoke two responses—a wistful nostalgia and a faint shudder. The shudder, of course, arises from the realization of how many hours of my childhood were wasted in front of the television watching mindless shows.

Over the years, as I have moved now into the middle part of my third decade, I have seen many improvements in technology: the microwave oven, the computer, the fax machine. Technology just keeps on improving.

As for television, when I grew up, we had the choice of all of three stations. Our set was a black and white, and we had to wait nearly a full minute for the tube to warm up. And when it did, the picture was none too great. Constant fiddling with the rabbit ears perched on top of the television only somewhat alleviated the frustration of an often wavy and fuzzy picture. Then, by the time I was in middle school, we had a color set with a much larger screen and we were hooked up to cable. We had seemingly endless choices of programming: some 22 channels. And things have continued to change. The TV set I now own has an even larger screen and the capacity to broadcast many of the stations in stereo sound. Our present cable system has nearly 75 different channels of programming, many of which broadcast around the clock.

Still, with all the variety that television offers today, it has not really improved that much from the days of my childhood. There is so much truth in Bruce Springsteen's song "67 Channels and Nothing On." And kids today still spend too many hours parked in front of the TV. This one-eyed bandit steals away their innocence and creativity and impairs their ability to think in a rational and concentrated manner. But before you write this chapter off as another diatribe against television ("heard it all before"), let me clarify my position.

I am not against television. I own a set and I watch it. I am not going to suggest that you throw the TV set away or take a hammer to it. I will not suggest that you go "cold turkey" and get rid of it. (Though if you find that, like many Americans, you are addicted to television, you might consider this option.) What I am suggesting is that you control your television viewing and that of your children. If you don't, it will control you in subtle and unpleasant ways. It can hamper the intellectual, creative, and spiritual development of your children and damage your family's communication and togetherness. Is this an extreme statement? I don't think so, and I'd like to offer some reasons why.

The Problem of Content

Certainly the most obvious problem with television is its content. Simply put, only a small portion of the available programs are suitable for family viewing. The newspaper *USA Today* did an interesting study. They watched one week of prime-time shows on the three major networks and Fox network in an attempt to find out whether TV reflects real life. Of 94 shows they watched:

48 showed at least one violent act.

There were a total of 276 acts of violence in which 57 people were killed and 99 seriously assaulted.

There were 45 sex scenes.

Of these 45 sex scenes:

23 were unmarried couples.
4 were between married heterosexuals.
1 involved a homosexual couple.
1 involved unmarried teens.

Compared to some of what I have seen, this research might have been conducted during a mild week. Other studies indicate that the average child watches up to 8,000 made-for-TV murders and 100,000 miscellaneous acts of violence by the time they reach the end of grade school.

And if the network television which supposedly must pass through network censors is like this, cable television is even worse. Between the degrading attitudes toward human sexuality daily broadcast on MTV and the explicit violence available at the push of the remote button, our children are assaulted with a constant barrage of negative messages from television.

Our children are in great danger of becoming morally desensitized. Perhaps the rampant and senseless violence now ravaging our nation is at least partly due to the fact that a generation of kids have grown up with a steady diet of murders and general mayhem on the screen. Perhaps the plague of illegitimacy that has robbed the innocence of so many young people is a reflection of the continual diet of sexually provocative images that are so much a part of our TV culture. Some of the commercials, with their teasing and leering provocations, are as dangerous as more explicit viewing.

The precious innocence of our children is bartered away for cheap entertainment and their moral sensibilities become shattered and crushed. After a repeated viewing of sex and violence on TV there comes a numbing effect. What we once found shocking and unthinkable becomes, at first, grudgingly accepted, and then later, embraced as normal and acceptable. Where once even the most tame expletive was unthinkable to us, we now listen to language on television that we would never allow anyone to use in our home. Our culture once held the sexual act in a place of sacred honor, but now on TV, it is routinely debased by leering references and an overall cheapness. The more excruciating forms of violence were once left to the viewer's imagination, but now we are exposed to them in bright technicolor.

Of course, some say the answer to this problem is simple. We simply control what we allow our children to watch. This certainly is important. We must constantly monitor what they are viewing if we want to protect their young minds from the onslaught of vile and degrading shows. I know one family that has written Philippians 4:8 on a card and posted it on the side of their television set.

> Finally, brothers, whatever is true, whatever is noble, whatever is right, whatever is pure, whatever is lovely, whatever is admirable—if anything is excellent or praiseworthy—think about such things.

Yes, controlling what you watch is important. But it is not the whole solution. How much and how often are also important issues, for television works on our psyches in many subtle and dangerous ways.

Television and Our Attention Spans

One primary concern about television is its effect on our attention spans. Something in the very nature of reading demands focus, concentration, and careful response. When we read a book we must focus our minds carefully if we want to understand and take in the message the author intends us to receive. Our imaginations must turn those small odd shapes (which we call letters) printed in black on the white paper into images and pictures in our minds. Reading exercises our brain power, forcing us to concentrate on the text before us and interact with it. Reading exercises our imaginations, forcing us to fill in the gaps, to imagine what a person or place might look like from the few clues the author gives us. When we are reading, we are in control. We can read faster or slower, we can pause and mentally argue a point with the author, we can add in thoughts from the fund of our own experience. It is, then, no wonder that children who read a great deal are generally smarter than children who read rarely. Even if the reading material is not of the highest quality or intellectual depth, the act of reading is in itself an exercise for our brains. One young man in my high school nourished himself largely on a steady diet of the cheapest and most predictable sort of pulp science fiction. It may not have influenced him in the way more intellectually stimulating books would have, but it still made him a formidable thinker. He could express himself well and he had an amazingly fertile imagination.

Watching television is a far different experience. Instead of words on the page, our mind is drawn to images which constantly change and shift. The average camera shot on network television lasts about 3.5 seconds. The eye never rests. Our minds are not given the opportunity to interact with the images. They come at us too thick and fast for us to respond. We are left to sit, zombielike, and take it in. The problem is that we just eat, we don't digest. It is like swallowing food without tasting it. One report suggests that 51 percent of viewers cannot remember even one item of news in any detail only a few minutes after the nightly news is over. It all parades in front of us—the sit-coms, the news, the dramas.

It takes little focus or concentration to watch TV. Of course, sometimes we all just need to "veg out" in front of the TV. But when we make it a habit, we begin to lose our focus and our ability to concentrate. Is it any wonder that the increase in television watching parallels the decline in school test scores?

Many parents and children alike find reading boring in comparison with television. But in reality, by any sane comparison, much of television is exceedingly boring. Many of the shows are tiresomely similar, predictable, and lacking in creativity. They are no match for the riches gained by reading a good book. Instead of challenging our imaginations, television settles for merely entertaining us.

Television and the Culture of Entertainment

On August 21, 1858, the first of a series of debates took place between Abraham Lincoln and Stephen Douglas. These debates were not set up for the purpose of getting elected to political office. At this time, neither of the men were running for the presidency or the Senate (though they did, of course, later). The debates were, instead, simply a forum for airing important political and social issues. Here was the format of the debate: Douglas would speak for one hour, and then, Lincoln would give a one-and-a-half hour response, followed by Douglas with a half-hour rebuttal. If this three-hour debate seems unusually long to you, in an earlier debate, Douglas gave a three-hour speech, after which the audience adjourned for dinner, and then returned for another four hours of Lincoln's response and more debating.

For us today, the idea that any audience would sit still for seven hours of closely argued debate is unthinkable. And yet, this was not uncommon in the days before television and moving pictures. Here was an audience, trained by reading, who had the ability to concentrate carefully, following closely argued points with relative ease. And the speakers were not so much interested in moving emotions as they were in convincing their audience intellectually. At one debate, Douglas made a point that drew wild and enthusiastic applause. He responded to the lengthy applause by saying, "My friends, silence will be more acceptable to me in the discussion of these questions than applause. I desire to address myself to your judgment, your understanding, and your consciences, and not to your passions and enthusiasms." Can you imagine any modern politician making such a statement? Now, many politicians are more concerned with image than with substance. The recent presidential debates are hardly worth comparing to the pure intellectual vigor of the Lincoln-Douglas debates. Our modern so-called debates are merely an opportunity for politicians to deliver a powerful "sound-bite" and to put across their carefully constructed image for their television audience. Television has trained us to expect politics to be entertaining.

Television has also taught us that religion should be entertaining. The antics of many of our media preachers are aimed at keeping easily bored audiences tuned in. They make little room or time for careful biblical exposition or theological reflection. The prime-time prophets must keep their audience entertained, and they often do it in the most embarrassing and questionable ways. The sermons of classic pulpiteers like Jonathan Edwards and Charles Spurgeon were based on carefully reasoned thinking and demanded attentive and patient audiences. Seldom would their sermons fit into the 20-minute time slot that is the norm for so many of our churches.

The emphasis on entertainment by the television age is also increasingly influencing our educational system. Shows like "Sesame Street" and "The Electric Company" do have some educational value, but is there not a danger that in trying to make learning fun, we are hiding an important truth: Learning takes effort. Learning does not happen by osmosis but by the expenditure of time, effort, and concentration. We mislead our kids when we give them the impression that education is all fun and games. They won't be able to depend on Kermit the Frog when they begin learning higher math, or struggle with the complexities of modern history. How can our schools possibly seem interesting to kids whose first exposure to learning is all done in songs, with puppets and cartoons to deliver the message? How can we get ideas across to children in Sunday school when we don't have the full range of audiovisual materials? Jesus did not say, "You shall be entertained by the truth and the truth shall set you free."

In the book *Amusing Ourselves to Death*, author Neil Postman explores how our modern obsession with entertaining images has destroyed what he calls the "typographic mind." By this, he means the mind that is trained and strengthened through reading. His fear is that we are developing into a culture of nonthinkers, who allow ourselves to be passively manipulated by the onslaught of images that come our way, and that we do not adequately engage our brains in public discourse because we would rather be entertained.

Television and Our Sense of the Real and Important

Too much exposure to television can warp our sense of what is truly important and valuable in life. The constant message coming at us on the screen is that success and happiness are measured by our net worth, by the amount and kind of toys we own. The commercials, in particular, by giving us a false definition of true happiness, create in us a greedy lust for ever-increasing consumption.

We are promised that we will have all the beautiful women or macho men we desire if only we drink the right beer, wear the right clothes, drive the right car, and eat the right kind of breakfast cereal. Happiness in TV land is defined by how well you stack up with the ideal man or woman. It requires money, the perfect body shape, and a healthy dose of "style." Few, if any of us, possess all three of these, and in the real world those who do possess them don't seem demonstrably happier or more well-adjusted than the rest of us. But TV builds a fantasy world where we can imagine ourselves the owners of all these qualities. It is a world where everyone is hip and funny. Those who are not are the comic foils. We find ourselves growing dissatisfied with the things in life that really do matter: character, faith, integrity, and peace of heart.

Television provides an edited and carefully chosen view of reality. We see only what the director or the cameraman wishes us to see, accompanied by music that manipulates our emotions, its swells and crescendos clueing us in to how we are supposed to feel about what we are seeing.

We live in the information age, and so we look to television also as a source of information. Nature shows, documentaries, talk shows, and especially the nightly news programs feed us all kinds of information day after day. But is it the kind of information we really need or can really use? The daily news becomes something like a soap opera, something we can tune into to catch the latest exciting wrinkles in our world, to give us something to talk about around the water cooler. Other than that, it has little effect on our lives, except perhaps the weather forecast (which few trust anyway).

The most life-transforming information is learned through experience. It is, for example, all well and good to pontificate about the tremendousness of God's grace. However, until we know it by experience within our own hearts and lives, it means little to us. The news report may inform us that certain people in our city or nation are homeless and lacking in the basic needs of existence. But does this fact do us any good if we can't or don't do anything about it? Because of its visual power, television can cause us to think and feel that we have experienced something when we have not. It is all mediated for us.

In his book *The Age of Missing Information*, Bill Kibben argues that television fails to inform us about what is really of importance in our everyday existence. He recounts an experiment he tried. On one day he recorded, with the help of many friends and video recorders, all 24 hours' worth of programming aired on all 93 available cable channels on the Fairfax Cable system, one of the largest in the nation. Over the next few months, he dutifully watched every moment of TV which was broadcast that day—more than 1,000 hours' worth. It was a grueling experience and it revealed much about the sad state of our society.

Later that summer, he spent a day camping out on a mountaintop by a small pond, not far from his home. Despite the multiplied hours of data in the documentaries and news reports he'd watched, he found that he learned much more of value for his life from one meditative day spent alone with nature in the woods. We are told, he points out, that television is a great and boundless source of information. He begs to differ:

> Against such a tide of opinion it sounds a little romantic to say: If you sat by a pond beside a hemlock tree under the sun and stars for a day, you might acquire some information that would serve you well. I don't fret about TV because it's decadent or shortens your attention span or leads to murder. It worries me because it alters perception. TV, and the culture it anchors, masks and drowns out the subtle and vital information contact with the real world once provided. There are lessons—small lessons, enormous lessons, lessons that may be crucial to the planet's persistence as a green and diverse place and also the happiness of its inhabitants—that nature teaches and TV can't. Subversive ideas about how much you need, or what comfort is, or beauty, or time, that you can learn from the one logoless channel and not the hundred noisy ones or even the pay-per-view.[1]

Try this experiement: Turn off the set and take a walk, read a book, have a family discussion. You'll be surprised at how little you will miss.

Television and the Preciousness of Our Time

How important is television in our culture? In 1990 it was found that 98 percent of all households in the United States owned at least one television set. Unthinkably, this is larger than the percentage of households which have indoor plumbing! What does that say about our priorities?

Twelve percent of all adults admit to being television addicts. About one in every eight people, that is, admits to a physical addiction to television. For them, it is a constant source of nourishment and sustenance; without it, they feel physical symptoms of withdrawal. Of course, as with all addictions, those who admit to their addiction are only a small percentage of those who actually depend on the addictive substance to get them through their days.

In 1960, the average daily viewing of television per household was 5.06 hours. By 1992 it had risen to 7.04 hours. (The average young child watches over 27 hours per week, or 4 hours a day.) In the average home this means that the set is on for nearly the entire evening, as well as at other times during the day. The average teenager spends a scant 1.8 hours a week reading, 5.6 hours a week on homework, and a whopping 21 hours watching television.

Think what it could mean if you could capture the time spent staring vacantly into an electronic box, and use it instead for valuable pursuits like family discussions, playing games, or reading aloud (or quietly) as a family.

There is no Frigate like a Book
To take us Lands away
Nor any Coursers like a Page
Of prancing Poetry—
This Traverse may the poorest take
Without oppress of Toll—
How Frugal is the Chariot
That bears the Human Soul.

—Emily Dickinson

•   •   •

12

The Adventure of Reading Aloud

Instilling a Love for Reading

*A*sk a group of adults and teens about their favorite memories from their early school years and many of them will mention the teacher reading aloud to them. For many of us, a favorite childhood memory is that time when we would snuggle up on the lap of mother, father, or a grandparent and listen as they read a book to us.

In earlier times the family would gather around the living room, perched in chairs or sprawling on the floor, while one member of the family read a book aloud to the others. Sometimes the family worked together (sewing, shelling nuts, shucking peas) while being entertained with a story. This family reading time was a source of valuable shared experiences, memories of warmth and togetherness and much entertainment, humor, and excitement. Unfortunately, this family tradition has become a casualty of the advent of the television in the home.

The Benefits of Reading

Reading is a mental activity which stretches us; the reading mind is engaged in contemplating, imagining, rereading, and responding. If we can cultivate in our children a love for books, they will go forth into the world with lively creativity, a hunger for knowledge, and the tools to grow intellectually and spiritually. Look for the leaders in almost any worthwhile endeavor, the people who are creative, intelligent, and spiritually mature, and you will find most of them are readers.

But statistics show that the average American reads less than one book per year. Only 50 percent of them have read a book in the last five years! An increasing number of people simply do not know how to read. Equally startling is the number of Christians who say they are committed to living their lives by the principles of Scripture but rarely spend any concentrated time reading the Bible. We have a culture-wide deficiency in the area of reading. As parents, we must commit ourselves to seeing that our children do not fall prey to this cultural trend.

Parents as Readers

We must provide an example for our children by our own reading habits. By our choice of reading material, we can show them that we value reading not only as entertainment, but also as a way of expanding our mind and learning new things. If they see that we as adults have a continuing desire to learn, they begin to understand that learning is a lifelong activity. For too many people, learning basically comes to an end when they graduate from high school or college. For some, the last time they read a serious book was while they were in school. We can demonstrate by our actions that this is not the case with us and that few things in life are as rewarding as learning something new.

Books: Furniture for the Home and Mind

Start to build a family library. The novelist Anthony Powell titled one of his novels *Books Do Furnish a Room*. I like that. I've always thought that a collection of books adds warmth and personality to a room. But bookcases full of books are not only beautiful furnishings for your home; they will also furnish your child's mind with valuable information, exciting stories, grand adventures, and spiritual nourishment. Have accessible places in your home where your child can go to explore the world of books. Of course, few of us will ever have an experience with books quite as rich as C. S. Lewis had, but listen to this delightful description of the place that books held in his childhood years.

> I am a product of long corridors, empty sunlit rooms, upstairs indoor silences, attics explored in solitude, distant noises of gurgling cisterns and pipes, and the noise of wind under the tiles. Also, of endless books. My father bought all the books he read and never got rid of any of them. There were books in the study, books in the drawing room, books in the cloakroom, books (two deep) in the great bookcase on the landing, books in a bedroom, books piled as high as my shoulder in the cistern attic, books of all kinds reflecting every transient stage of my parent's interest, books readable and unreadable, books suitable for a child and books most emphatically not. Nothing was forbidden me. In the seemingly endless rainy afternoons I took volume after volume from the shelves. I had always the same certainty of finding a book that was new to me as a man who walks into a field has of finding a new blade of grass.[2]

If we can provide an environment of books that is even half as magical as this one, we have given our children a rich treasure.

Reading Aloud

A 1985 report of the United States Government Commission on Reading came to this conclusion: "The single most important activity for building the knowledge required for eventual success in reading is reading aloud to children." A U.S. Department of Education publication entitled *What Works: Research About Teaching and Learning*, says simply: "The best way for parents to help their children become better readers is to read to them—even when they are very young."

Begin early with simple books like the delightful *Goodnight Moon* by Margaret Wise Brown. My children would ask me to read this book night after night just before bedtime. It had a wonderfully soothing and calming effect which prepared them well for the night's sleep. This book and others like it introduce to our kids the idea that books are something special.

As they grow older, expand the reading. In our family we have read collections of fairy tales, *The Chronicles of Narnia*, stories by George MacDonald, *Little Women*, Greek myths (great for demonstrating moral virtues and vices in action), *Tom's Midnight Garden*, biographies, nature books and, of course, the Bible. My children tend to get very upset when something interrupts or prevents the evening ritual of family reading.

One of the difficulties for those parents who were not themselves readers is finding good books to read. Much of what is available for kids is simply not good. Many children's books are tedious and boring, especially those designed for first readers. It is no wonder that children often do not learn a love for reading. So choose books with humor and excitement, not those which are overly moralistic or those which are based on the latest cartoons and movies—these are usually poorly written and lacking in creativity. Since books are one way in which your children learn about the world, make sure that what they are reading is honest, realistic, and morally responsible. To help you get started I have included an annotated list of reading material for the family at the end of this book. Of course, these are not the only good books, but over time they have proven themselves. Most of them could justifiably be called classics. For further reading suggestions you might consult *Honey for a Child's Heart* (Gladys Hunt), *For Reading Out Loud* (Margaret Mary Kimmel and Elizabeth Segel), or Jim Trelease's *Read-Aloud Handbook*.

Continue to read aloud to your children once they are old enough to read for themselves. They will still enjoy sitting spellbound as a good story unravels. You can introduce them to books they may not yet have the skill to read themselves but which are well worth knowing. By reading to them, you can continue to create family togetherness. Also, the more you read together as a family, the more they will continue reading for themselves, on their own. Finally, you will reinforce the idea that reading is fun for adults as well as children, and is an experience which can continue throughout their lives.

If your older children are reluctant to sit still for a story—especially if this is a new experience for your family—you must win them over by choosing books to fit their interests and then being realistic about how much time they are able to sit still. I think you will find that they can quickly be won over to this delightful activity. Perhaps a family vacation or a long car trip is the time to start. Our family has enjoyed many a story while traveling. On a recent trip, my wife raced against the setting sun to finish reading *The Reluctant Dragon* to us. We all wanted to hear the ending, so she finished by flashlight. You might also want to try a well-read book on tape. A book helps the time pass for both driver and passengers.

Putting It Into Practice

Here are some helpful tips for reading aloud:

1. *It takes practice to be a good reader.* Don't expect to be an expert overnight. The more you read aloud, the better you'll get at it. Don't be discouraged if your first attempts are halting and imperfect. Keep at it, you'll improve.

2. *Put life into the story by expressive reading.* If you can, use a different voice or inflection for each character. Don't overdo this if there are a lot of characters though. Both you and your listener will get confused! You might want to read the story ahead of time to yourself, so that you can build in drama and expression. Have fun. Be a little crazy.

3. *Read with clear enunciation.* Say the words clearly and slowly enough that they can be understood. Don't rush, but don't go too slowly either or you might lose their attention.

4. *Start with short readings and work up to longer ones.* Don't read so much at one sitting that the children start to squirm and complain. Leave them wanting more.

5. *Pick a quiet time and place for reading.* Try to minimize distractions by carefully choosing your location and time for reading. Usually the evenings, just before bedtime, work best for most families. But other times, including car trips, can be enjoyable as well.

6. *As the athletic shoe commercial says: Just Do It.* Don't wait for the perfect time, the perfect book, or the perfect reading ability. Just have fun. Reading aloud to your children is fun, rewarding, educational and, best of all, it will draw you closer together as a family.

But supposing that by casting all these things into an imaginary world, stripping them of their stained glass and Sunday school associations, one could make them for the first time appear in their real potency? Could one not thus steal past those watchful dragons?

—C. S. Lewis

· · ·

13

The Moral Value of Stories

Stories as Moral Teachers

*T*here is little need to trot out statistics or give examples which point to the near collapse of moral values in our culture: moral irresponsibility, drug abuse, senseless violence, sexual perversion, greed, and many other things we could name. The daily newspaper tells the story. So does even a cursory glance at what we call "entertainment." Much of our entertainment is aimed at satisfying the fleeting desires of the moment and keeping our boredom at bay; it often neither challenges us nor attempts to change us, but only reinforces our own failings and weaknesses.

As a society, we do not work hard to instill moral values. Too often, instead of encouraging one another to choose and act morally, we create ways that make such choices unnecessary by removing the consequences of immoral behavior.

T. S. Eliot wrote that modern thinkers spend a lot of time "dreaming up systems so perfect that no one will need to be good." This is perfectly illustrated by the recent emphasis on condom education rather than abstinence education. We just assume that our young people could not possibly control their sexual appetites. The reason behind this is that we suffer from a culture-wide lack of moral vision. Not only do our children not seem capable of practicing the virtues, they often cannot even define them (ask a young person what *chastity* or *prudence* means). And then, not only can they not practice or define them, but they generally do not even see them as a goal worth pursuing. They cannot recognize them in action and do not see how exercising them could improve their lives. After all, moral values are hard to practice, they cost something, and they do not provide immediate gratification. In other words, modern young people have failed to capture a vision for these values. They do not possess a "moral imagination."

The challenge which faces us, then, is how to instill a moral vision in our children and in ourselves. How do we cultivate a view of life and of the world which enables us to respond to life in a morally creative way? How do we instill in our children the ability to act morally? One way to help children develop a moral imagination is through the reading and telling of stories.

How Stories Transform Us

For some of us, the idea that stories could help us develop our moral values is a foreign one. Many of us have "learned" moral values by memorizing lists of moral directives. How could stories move us to moral action or change our moral perspective? This is possible because stories can reflect real life more than abstract teaching can. William Kilpatrick has written,

> Life is rich and full and complex like a story, not abstract and neat like a theory. The things that happen to us—the

> great joys, the intense sorrows, the surging passions—
> are too much like drama to be accounted for by anything
> less than drama.... Unless the moral imagination is
> hooked, the other moral faculties—will, emotion, and
> reason—are too often over-matched by fear, laziness,
> and self-interest.[1]

Literature, then, does not merely tell us about an experience, but rather presents experiences as living realities.

Every part of our being needs to be transformed and converted. Abstract truth, through argumentation and logical thinking, can reach the mind and change it. But just knowing what we *should* do is not enough. The difficult part of morality is actually doing what we know we should do. The problem is not only with the intellect, but also with the will. The imagination is profoundly connected to the will. If we can imagine the right response, we are on our way to making it. If we can imagine what doing the right thing might look like, we have made a large step toward choosing it. Stories help us develop a *moral* imagination, an imagination we can use in the service of doing good and in being a good person. These are several ways stories can help us to learn moral values.

1. *Stories allow us to expand our range of experiences.*

Fiction allows us a wider range of experiences than life would otherwise send our way. We might never experience travel in far-off lands, the thrill of achieving a seemingly impossible goal, the terror of being pursued by those with evil intent, or the joy of finding riches beyond our imagining. We certainly cannot journey back in time to the Middle Ages to cross swords with a Black Knight or wander with a traveling troubadour. Most of us will never experience the thrill and fear of space travel or come face-to-face with unimaginable horror. Yet, through the pages of a well-written story, all of these experiences become available to us. We can experience them vicariously.

Growth in character comes mainly through our experiences. Our personalities are deepened and we grow in wisdom. The art of writing is the art of composing experience. The writer must select significant details and write of them in such a way that the reader shares in the experience. How well these details are chosen and narrated determines how thoroughly we are convinced and moved by a story. If the author has done the job well, we will feel the racing of the pulse, the shortness of breath, the exalted realization, the passion, or the all-engulfing sense of romantic attachment that the character in the story is experiencing. These feelings, emotions, and realizations provide opportunities for our hearts and minds to grow.

Of course, some experiences may be dangerous to experience vicariously. Perverse sexuality or gratuitous violence, for example, may breed a fascination and preoccupation with evil. Stories with these themes may simply gratify our twisted desires rather than provide opportunity to broaden our experiences. When we cross this delicate line, we may do damage to our spirits. But to depict sin in a story is not necessarily to advocate it. A story without evil actions is a pale and unrealistic tale indeed.

2. *Stories exercise our "moral muscles."*

In well-written fiction, difficult and complex moral situations are brought before us which cause us to have to make some sort of moral judgment. Like our physical bodies, our moral senses require exercise and training so that we are capable of dealing with circumstances that require moral courage and stamina. An athlete must condition himself with constant practice, building the strength that will enable him to respond correctly in a given athletic situation and developing the necessary stamina to achieve his goals. When we vicariously experience moral quandaries and difficult situations in books, our moral muscles become "toned." Then, when we are called upon to make judgments in the context of our daily lives, we are more prepared to make them wisely.

3. *Stories help us to grow in moral sensitivity.*

When we project ourselves into someone else's feelings and experiences, we learn to empathize with them. It is difficult to identify with another's hardships when they lie outside our own experience. The multiplying experiences we read about in literature give us the opportunity to empathize, to feel with the pains and humiliations of the characters. Hopefully, this will teach us compassion for those around us who suffer in actual life. If we have our heart broken by Anne Frank's suffering, perhaps we can also have our heart broken by the sufferings of those around us.

4. *Stories provide us with a powerful vision of goodness.*

The philosopher Alfred North Whitehead once said that "moral education is impossible apart from the habitual vision of greatness." Children must carry a constant vision for the possibility of good in themselves. Children, like the rest of us, are sinners. Sometimes we fail to recognize how deep their awareness of their own moral imperfection is. In fact, true goodness seems almost impossible to some children, so aware are they of the darkness within them. A story's portrayal of goodness can give children the hope that they, like the characters in the story, can rise above their darkness and do what is right.

In an age in which we have debunked many of our heroes, we need to see examples of moral heroism in action. Biographies are one way of putting these examples before our eyes, as are fictional stories. They show us possibilities for courageous moral action and provide us with visions of the fascinating character of goodness.

5. *Stories help us see ourselves as we really are.*

Sometimes we get so wrapped up in our own personal lives that we cannot see our actions and attitudes for what they are. Stories help us see ourselves objectively. As George Bernard Shaw has written, "You use a glass mirror to see your face; you use works of art to see your soul."

Within the pages of Scripture we see a powerful example of how stories can bring us face to face with the evasions and deceits in our own lives. An event in 2 Samuel 11 and 12 stands out. It is a time of war, and many of the men of Jerusalem are away from their homes, fighting at the front. King David is on the roof of his palace when he spies young Bathsheba bathing. Struck by her beauty, he uses his royal prerogatives and arranges a sexual liaison with her. A short time later he discovers she is pregnant. Hoping to cover his tracks, David has her husband, Uriah, recalled from the war for a furlough, fully expecting that the man and wife will enjoy their marital pleasures. That way, when the baby arrives there will be no awkward questions. Everyone will assume it is Uriah's child. David has, however, underestimated Uriah's loyalty to duty. Instead of sleeping with his wife, he sleeps at the palace door. The next night, David attempts to get Uriah drunk and shake loose his resolve. This also fails. Finally, in frustration, David has Uriah posted at a vulnerable position at the front of the battle where he is sure to be killed. Sure enough, an enemy arrow strikes him down. David thinks his "problem" is solved when he marries Bathsheba soon after.

This is not the end of his problem, however, for the prophet Nathan comes to him to tell him a story. Had Nathan come with a straightforward rebuke, David might have dismissed him and his words in anger. Nathan might have ended up in prison, or at best, escorted quickly from the palace. But Nathan knew that David's heart was soft at its core and that he must reach him through his heart. So Nathan told his king this story:

> There were two men in a certain town, one rich and the other poor. The rich man had a very large number of sheep and cattle, but the poor man had nothing except one little ewe lamb he had bought. He raised it, and it grew up with him and his children. It shared his food, drank from his cup and even slept in his arms. It was like a daughter to him.
>
> Now a traveler came to the rich man, but the rich man refrained from taking one of his own sheep or cattle to

prepare a meal for the traveler who had come to him. Instead he took the ewe lamb that belonged to the poor man and prepared it for the one who had come to him (2 Samuel 12:1-4).

You can imagine the series of emotions which must have passed through David's mind: curiosity about the story, a tender sentimental feeling for the man and his beloved lamb, and then a growing sense of indignation at the actions of the unjust rich man. Finally, he exploded in anger: "As surely as the Lord lives, the man who did this deserves to die!"

Nathan looked steadily into the eyes of David and spoke with an intensity born of conviction, "You are the man." In a moment of revelatory insight, David finally perceived the great wrong he had done. Undoubtedly, up to this time he had managed to justify his actions and attitudes, or at least to ignore the enormity of his sin. *After all,* he probably told himself, *what's done is done . . . he probably would have died in battle anyway . . . maybe God intended for me and Bathsheba to be together. . . .* Now suddenly he saw through his self-deceit and saw his actions clearly for what they were. Though his mind was able to dream up justifications, his heart knew the truth. Through the story, Nathan captured David's heart and caused him to finally see himself as he appeared from the outside. "I have sinned," David said.

The Power of Stories

A story can penetrate to the deepest levels of our being. It can challenge our immorality. It can provide models for truly heroic ethical behavior. It can show us the right road to travel.

Traditional cultures have always used epics, stories, and fairy tales to pass on their cultural values. Our culture is no different. But modern educators and parents are no longer using these forms effectively, and instead are choosing to allow television and popular music to fill that role. Television sit-coms and MTV are taking the place of great literature in shaping many a child's moral values. But most parents, if they stop and think about it, would probably be quick to recognize the enormous difference in moral vision between Hollywood's attitudes and their own values.

Nietzsche was right when he suggested that people are more easily moved by beauty than by argument. Our aesthetic sense, when aroused, can significantly shape our views of the world. Hitler used this truth very effectively. By wrapping his vision for Germany in theatricality and splendid ceremony, he was able to draw into his view of things those who would be repulsed at his ideas were they stated in a simple didactic manner. People are drawn to a fully formed view of existence which can be articulated with beauty and vigor.

One of the great failings of modern evangelical Christianity is our inability to attract people to our *vision* of life. Great art can speak volumes, but we rely so often only on rational argument. What art and literature we do produce tends to be blandly propagandistic. Fiction that is too didactic loses its power as fiction. A good story speaks for itself and leaves room for us to discover the truth for ourselves. For example, the unusual power of the portrayal of Aslan in C. S. Lewis' *The Chronicles of Narnia* is that it is not simply a bland one-for-one allegory of faith. Aslan does not simply appear as Jesus in disguise. Instead, as we read, we are drawn to this character and it slowly dawns on us that this is what Christ would be like in this other world. The joy comes from the discovery. Suddenly, the truth blazes into flame before our eyes on the printed page—our values became not an abstract truth, but *the* truth.

Our values receive their most powerful evocation when we can present them in a story, giving them what Alistair MacIntyre sees as an essential narrative structure. In his book *After Virtue*, he writes,

> Deprive children of stories and you leave them unscripted, anxious stutterers in their actions as in their words. Hence there is no way to give us understanding of any society, including our own, except through the stock of

stories which constitute its dramatic resources. Mythology, in its original sense, is at the heart of things. Vico was right and so was Joyce. And so too is that moral tradition from heroic society to its medieval heirs according to which the telling of stories has a key part in educating us into the virtues.[2]

When rational thought confronts us, we are forced to either reckon with it or ignore it. But stories give us room to breathe. They have the ability to sneak up behind us and draw us in. They touch us in our hearts, in our places of vulnerability. They catch us off guard and leap past our defenses.

Plato's goal for the youth of his ideal republic was that they might develop an "erotic attachment" to virtue; that they might have a passionate desire for living virtuous lives, that they might find the life of virtue exciting and worthy of exemplification. Ultimately, morality is not rule-keeping, but role-playing. Great literature can provide our children with models of ethical behavior that will inspire them and challenge them to view their own lives and behavior differently. Stories and biographies show children moral values in action.

The mythical tale of Abraham Lincoln walking three miles to return six cents provides a model of honesty, as Aesop's "The Boy Who Cried Wolf" shows the danger inherent in lying. *The Diary of Anne Frank*, *King Lear*, and Dickens' *A Christmas Carol* all demonstrate both the need for compassion and the possibility of reaching out to those less fortunate. The great stories of our civilization are full of moral lessons. "Beauty and the Beast" teaches us to look beyond the external to find inner quality. The Greek myth of Pandora's box demonstrates the danger of unchecked curiosity. *The Odyssey* demonstrates qualities of courage, loyalty, and fidelity, all employed by characters who are morally imperfect. *Little Women* teaches us about the beauty of family life and the need to deal with our own personal shortcomings. Books like C. S. Lewis' *The Chronicles of Narnia* make the principles of the spiritual world more real to children, and Aslan presents a vivid image of the goodness and majesty of God. On and on the list could go.

Once we recognize the relationship between moral virtue and moral vision, it becomes clear that often a story is the most effective way to stimulate the moral centers within our children. A story first draws them in, then captures their interest and imagination, and finally, subtly, begins the process of transformation. Is it then any wonder that Jesus Himself did most of His teaching through the telling of stories? As parents we must fill the minds of our children with good stories, novels, fairy tales, biographies, myths, and Bible stories, so that they might have the tools to cultivate a moral imagination—the ability to think creatively and heroically in the moral realm.

[In art] the fundamental idea seems to be the revelation of the true through the beautiful.

—George MacDonald

. . .

14

The True
and the Beautiful

*A Christian Perspective
on the Importance of the Arts*

*R*ecently, I had the opportunity to spend the better part of a day in the Metropolitan Museum of Art in New York City. I wandered among the original paintings of Rembrandt, Van Gogh, Picasso, and Seurat, recognizing works I had previously only known from photos in books or cheap reproductions. I marveled at the mysterious simplicity and power of the collection of icons and early religious paintings, stood in awe before massive Renaissance canvases, and was transfixed by the beauty of landscape paintings from the nineteenth century. I paused and shook my head over the impenetrability of some of the modern works. As a believer, I marveled at the insight into the glory of creation and the fallenness of humanity which this magnificent collection of works divulged.

I stopped to chat with one of the guards, who told me about his adventures in guarding these priceless treasures. It was obvious that he took a great deal of pride in his job and did not underestimate its importance. He had come to love the works that he protected from inquisitive fingers or thoughtless vandals. He knew these were priceless human treasures. Truly they were irreplaceable, but how should I view them as a Christian?

The experiences and revelations in my heart and spirit during that day in the museum only confirmed the way I already felt about great art and its power to enrich the life of any human being. I also thought, with pleasure, that my children would not grow up to be artistically illiterate; my wife and I have taken pains to expose our two girls to fine art, music, and literature. And we have discovered that the introduction of great art into the lives of our children has awakened within them a sense of beauty and proportion, of fine sensibility and discernment.

The suggestion that a love for the arts can further a child's emotional, intellectual, and spiritual maturity will be suspect to some parents. An appreciation for the arts is seen as a purely leisure activity, certainly enjoyable and sometimes entertaining, but not really that important. This attitude toward the arts is, unfortunately, pervasive in the evangelical community. While willing to admit that the arts can be useful at times (in evangelism, for instance), many do not see them as anything more than frivolous embroidery on the fabric of daily life. But the arts are far more than just a way to kill time, unwind, and relax after the more pressing duties of daily living; they are enriching, ennobling, and expanding.

Because we don't see the arts as important, it is not surprising that much of our "Christian art" is of the most shallow and forgettable sort. With this attitude, it is also not surprising that many Christians feel that art needs some sort of justification. Unless it is useful in evangelism, some say, it is ultimately a waste of time. Some believers point to the dictum of Matthew Arnold that art would eventually replace religion and ask if indeed that usurpation has not already occurred. It is true that many who would never darken the doors of a church building will gaze in awe and wonder at the paintings in an art gallery, or close their eyes in ecstasy at a symphonic concert. And along with the tendency to idolize art, the reality is that much of what currently goes by the name of art is vulgar, tasteless, or entirely impenetrable to any but the "initiated." Many modern artists glory in the elitism of producing work that only a handful of the artistic cognoscente can understand or appreciate. With these realities, is it surprising that some Christians are quick to dismiss an emphasis on the arts as elitist, frivolous, and ultimately unspiritual?

I would, however, like to challenge this conclusion about the arts and point to some of the reasons why they are so important for the intellectual, emotional, and spiritual growth of our children.

Art Needs No Justification

We are a culture of utilitarians. We seem to feel the urgency to find a practical value for everything, to measure the hours consumed by every activity and point to its pragmatic value to us. That we should even ask the question, "What are art and beauty good for?" is a sign of the spiritual poverty of our age, and of the church which so often demands concrete, measurable results for every expenditure of time, effort, and money.

Hans Rookmaker, the late art historian and a colleague of Francis Schaeffer, said it well in the title of a small book he wrote: *Art Needs No Justification*. And while this is so very true, one feels compelled to justify it before those who dismiss it as merely a form of entertainment or as a distraction from the more essential endeavors of life.

Creativity: God's Nature and Ours

Genesis 1:27 tells us that we are created in the image of God. Of course, theologians have long debated precisely what this means. Certainly one characteristic of God's image is found in our drive toward creativity. The creation of the universe is the first act of God recorded in the Scriptures. By His word alone, by His creative will, God brought the world into existence. But His creativity did not stop there. In fact, God's ongoing creativity can be seen in the lives of His children. Ephesians 2:10 says, "For we are God's workmanship, created in Christ Jesus to do good works, which God prepared in advance for us to do." The Greek word for "workmanship" is *poiema,* the word that comes down to us in English as *poem.* We are, this verse tells us, God's poem. The same God whose creative energies brought the worlds into being is working in our lives to transform us into the type of people He wants us to be.

Human beings share in a small way in the reality of creation. Although we cannot speak worlds into existence or even cause a tree to come into being, we can produce beautiful things: paintings, sculptures, crafts, beautiful music or poetry. Dorothy Sayers says this in her book *The Mind of the Maker*:

> How then can [man] be said to resemble God? Is it his immortal soul, his rationality, his self-consciousness, his free will, or what, that gives him a claim to this rather startling distinction? A case may be argued for all these elements in the complex nature of man. But had the author of Genesis anything particular in mind when he wrote? It is observable that in the passage leading up to the statement about man, he has given no detailed information about God. Looking at man, he sees in him something essentially divine, but when we turn back to see what he says about the original upon which the "image" of God was modeled, we find only the single assertion, "God created." The characteristic common to God and man is apparently that: the desire and ability to make things.[1]

Few things in life bring us more joy and fulfillment than when our imaginations can transpose our thoughts and impressions into a reality which we can share with others. The refrigerator in our home is the "art gallery," and my children take great pride in displaying there the fruit of their creativity. Sometimes it is difficult to remove a quart of milk from the fridge without causing a cascade of paintings, drawings, sketches, and notes to come tumbling down. But it is important that my children have a place to display their work, for sharing the results of our creative efforts is half the joy. Recently, both of my daughters won awards at the county fair for their drawings. We framed and matted one of the best drawings which each of them had done. Oh, the looks on their faces when they saw their drawings displayed there in public view and adorned with the ribbons which showed that others had judged their work worthy of honor.

Because God knows how fulfilling this process of creating can be, and because in His love He prizes the expressions of our deepest thoughts and feelings and the hard work it takes to transform them into a work of art, the Bible is full of examples of fine art fashioned for the glory of God. The Bible mentions just about every kind of art or craft that exists. In the adornment of the temple, God called for the work of metallurgists, sculptors, painters, weavers, architects, and many others. To God this artistic work was so important that He called certain people to execute it. The Lord called Belazel to be an artist (Exodus 35:30). It was (and still is) a vocation from God. And the art for the temple was not all utilitarian. Much of it was purely for adornment—a wonderful, breathtaking, frivolous excess. For God revels in beauty and so should we!

An Inner Sanctuary of Peace and Order

Art helps keep us focused on that which is truly beautiful and good. The poet Wordsworth wrote that the mind should be "a mansion for all lovely forms." Philippians 4:8 calls us to focus on that which is true, noble, pure, lovely, and admirable. The vision of beauty available to us in great art is something we can carry with us into the chaos and disorder of our lives. Sometimes we are driven from one activity to the next by the momentum of necessity and spend our whole life missing out on the enjoyment of the present moment. Both God's creation (nature) and human creation (the arts) provide us with islands of peace and beauty that can nourish us in the midst of the squalor and ugliness of man's fallen world. Often a poem or a painting, whether read or recollected, can cause us to slow down and refocus on what truly matters in our lives. William Wordsworth captures his own experience of beauty in his poem "I Wandered Lonely as a Cloud":

> I wandered lonely as a cloud
> That floats on high o'er vales and hills,
> When all at once I saw a crowd,
> A host, of golden daffodils;
> Beside the lake, beneath the trees,
> Fluttering and dancing in the breeze.
>
> Continuous as the stars that shine
> And twinkle on the milky way,
> They stretched in never-ending line
> Along the margin of a bay:
> Ten thousand saw I at a glance,
> Tossing their heads in sprightly dance.
>
> The waves beside them danced; but they
> Out-did the sparkling waves in glee:
> A poet could not but be gay,
> In such a jocund company:
> I gazed—and gazed—but little thought
> What wealth the show to me had brought:
>
> For oft, when on my couch I lie
> In vacant or in pensive mood,
> They flash upon that inward eye,
> Which is the bliss of solitude;
> And then my heart with pleasure fills,
> And dances with the daffodils.

After a difficult day of distractions and frustrations, of hurrying and worrying, I can sit with a poem by Wordsworth, or maybe Gerard Manley Hopkins, T. S. Eliot, or Czeslaw Milocz and be refocused, reenergized, and prepared to cope again with the realities of life. At other times a Beethoven string quartet, one of Bach's Brandenburg concertos or Schubert's Trout Quintet is the healing element. Or maybe the perusal of a book of prints of the paintings of Caravaggio, Rembrandt, or Vermeer. "Beauty," writes George Mac-Donald, "is one of the surest antidotes to vexation. Often when life looked dreary about me, from some real or fancied injustice or indignation, has a thought of truth been flashed into my mind from a flower, a shape of frost, or even a lingering shadow, —not to mention such glories as angel-winged clouds, rainbows, stars, and sunrises."[2]

Great art gives us a special kind of life-affirming pleasure simply not available in the pallid fare of television or top-40 music. If we will introduce our children to the exquisite pleasures of truly fine art, we will give them a magnificent source for creating more fulfilling lives.

Training the Inward Eye

Art trains the inward eye. It helps us see more deeply and clearly into the realities of our everyday life. It awakens our senses, and as a result, we look more searchingly into ourselves and the world which surrounds us. Too often we miss the gratuitous grace of God. Annie Dillard illustrates this in a passage from her book *A Pilgrim at Tinker Creek*:

> When I was six or seven years old, growing up in Pittsburgh, I used to take a precious penny of my own and hide it for someone else to find. It was a curious compulsion; sadly, I've never been seized by it since. For some reason I always "hid" the penny along the same stretch of sidewalk up the street. I would cradle it at the roots of a sycamore, say, or in a hole left by a chipped-off piece of sidewalk. Then I would take a piece of chalk, and, starting at either end of the block, draw huge arrows leading up to the penny from both directions. After I learned to

write, I labeled the arrows: SURPRISE AHEAD or MONEY THIS WAY. I was greatly excited, during all this arrow-drawing, at the thought of the first lucky passerby who would receive in this way, regardless of merit, a free gift from the universe. But I never lurked about, I would go straight home and not give the matter another thought, until some months later, I would be gripped again by the impulse to hide another penny.

It is still the first week in January, and I've got great plans. I've been thinking about seeing. There are lots of things to see, unwrapped gifts and free surprises. The world is fairly studded and strewn with pennies cast broadside from a generous hand. But—and this is the point—who gets excited by a mere penny? If you follow one arrow, if you crouch motionless on a bank to watch a tremulous ripple thrill on the water and are rewarded by the sight of a muskrat kit paddling from its den, will you count that ship a chip of copper only, and go your rueful way? It is dire poverty indeed when a man is so malnourished and fatigued that he won't stoop to pick up a penny. But if you cultivate a healthy poverty and simplicity, so that finding a penny will literally make your day, then, since the world is in fact planted in pennies, you have with your poverty bought a lifetime of days. It is that simple. What you see is what you get.[3]

How blind we can sometimes be to the sacredness of the ordinary. Would that we could, with William Blake,

> . . . see a world in a grain of sand
> And heaven in a wild flower,
> Hold infinity in the palm of your hand
> And eternity in an hour.

In our culture, we tend to use art as a diversion, a leisure activity, a time-filler. Therefore, the art that is the most popular is the art that is the least demanding. But the truest art gives us eyes to see more deeply into ourselves and into the world around us. Great art often functions like a shock of cold water across our face.

In our scientific society we focus on the outward appearances of things, on what our senses can interact with. We try to reduce life to the rational sphere, pretending that everything can be rationally dissected, examined, and explained. But it cannot. And art reminds us of this truth.

> God save us from the thoughts men think
> In the mind alone,
> He that sings a lasting song
> Thinks in a marrow bone.
>
> (William B. Yeats)

Art is a reaching after transcendence. It is the probing of the mysteries of life. It awakens the senses. It grips the spirit. It brings us alive. It causes us to see. Art is a bridge between the natural and the spiritual realms; it forces us to see that there is more to life than that which meets our physical eyes.

Training Our Sensibilities

Art not only trains the eye, but also trains the sensibilities. It confronts us with new insights and experiences, and also causes us to feel more deeply. Our lives are made up of a limited number of experiences. Great art takes us beyond this limitation and exercises our emotions. It trains our sensitivities and sympathies. For example, in the comfort of our personal experience, we might never come into contact with real poverty. We might see it on the evening news. Or we might glimpse from the safety of our car the poor, unfortunate person standing on the sidewalk holding a sign which reads "Will work for food." But great novels like Victor Hugo's *Les Miserables* and Dickens' *Hard Times* bring the reality directly before us by involving us in the very lives of the poor and downtrodden. We are given the opportunity in these works to feel the depth of the characters' despair and sorrow. If the impact of great art fails to touch us deeply, then it shows that we have become hardened. As William Shakespeare recognized,

The man that hath no music in himself,
Nor is moved with concord of sweet sounds,
Is fit for treasons, stratagems, and spoils,
The motions of his spirit are dull as night,
And his affections dark as Erebus.
Let no such man be trusted. Mark the music.

(The Merchant of Venice)

Shakespeare is pointing here to a connection between cultural appreciation and character. The man who cannot appreciate the beauties of music is a man, he says, who cannot be trusted. Shakespeare is not alone in viewing art this way. It is a truism that refined taste is often, though not always, a mark of character. We speak sometimes of developing "taste." Developing "taste" means learning to appreciate what is truly good. This does not happen automatically. It takes effort and education. More than anything else, it takes exposure. The average top-40 single on popular radio can usually be enjoyed immediately. One or two listenings are often sufficient to get a grasp of the song; but it takes many listenings and some effort to fully appreciate a Beethoven string quartet. And you can return again and again to the Beethoven piece for refreshment and an experience of beauty. The qualities of the pop song, on the other hand, are often quickly exhausted. It will have dropped off the charts after a few weeks, forgotten except for the occasional moment of nostalgia. In other artistic forms we see this same principle at work. It takes more effort to fully appreciate a painting by Rembrandt than it does a child's scrawl or a cartoon from the Sunday newspaper.

Of course, discipline is necessary to get a full vision of the good. In the moral sphere, that which is natural and immediate is often not that which is righteous and good. As in the artistic realm, moral values are a matter of exposure, discipline, hard work, and ultimately, joy. It is part of our responsibility as parents to teach our children to like what is good, to direct their emotions in a way that's healthy and productive.

Too often as Christians we judge a work only by its content. If, for example, a song or a novel effectively presents the gospel, we judge it good. But this does not really encompass what the arts are all about. In the arts there is a difference between form and content. Content is the message of the work of art, its message about the meaning of life. Form is the way in which that message is crafted, the workmanship that goes into making it communicate effectively and please the viewer aesthetically. Sometimes it happens that we immediately respond to the content without noting the shoddy form. Sometimes we appreciate the marvelous form even though we cannot fully agree with the worldview implicit in its content. Good art necessitates quality of execution in its chosen form.

Art and Sentimentality

A certain kind of art exercises the emotions, but does so in the wrong way. It reduces real emotion to "sentimentality." This kind of art does not promote moral training because it merely works at our feelings without any real vision of the moral good involved. It uses all the old tricks to get our emotions stirred. It appeals to the sentiments and the emotions without having excellence of form. This kind of art is called "kitsch." Webster defines *kitsch* as "artistic or literary material of low quality designed to appeal to current popular taste." Kitsch takes grand themes and emotions and reduces them to a formula, such as the average popular love song or the tearjerker movie. It seeks to push the right buttons in us and manipulate us into a response. It trivializes sentiments which are genuinely deep by going for the formulaic appeal. It gratifies desires without offering anything of value in its wake. It uses cheap effects to numb its audience and get us to respond emotionally. We are not called to reflect on the experiences it portrays, only to respond to them. It narrows our experiences rather than widening them because it is without ambiguity.

Kitsch also involves giving people what they want. As the novelist Milan Kundera has written, "Kitsch excludes everything from its purview which is essentially unacceptable in human existence." It denies the pain, the struggle, and loss that are a part of human existence, and we are left with a sanitized, everything-is-all-right, Disney-style "happy ending" approach to life. Ultimately kitsch is a denial of reality and of the biblical doctrine of human fallenness. Unfortunately, many of our modern Christian "works of art" suffer from these characteristics, causing complacency, satisfaction with our smug religiosity, denial of the dark side of existence.

Great art helps us become more realistic about our sinfulness and weaknesses. It forces us to face the important questions of life. It tweaks our comfortableness and reveals the hidden motives of even the best actions. It can cause us to fall in honesty on our face before the living God.

Art and the Christian Vision

If we can fill the lives of our children with the great art of our Christian heritage, we can instill in them a moral vision of reality. Everyone has a particular view of reality, and this "worldview" determines how we make judgments and discern truth. Some people think a worldview is only an intellectual framework, a group of rational and personal presuppositions. But this is far too limiting. We are not just thinking machines. Our actions and thoughts are certainly affected by more than our mental perceptions. And so our worldview includes our theology and philosophy. While it is indeed our intellectual presuppositions, it is also our feelings, our attitudes, and our motivations. It is, more fundamentally, the way we interpret the experiences of our lives. Art can help us with this process.

A work of art is an interpretation of reality. The artist impresses upon us the way that he or she sees the world. When we look at, read, or listen to a work of art, we are confronted not with reality itself but with an interpretation of reality. The artist takes the mass of sense experience and distills it for our pleasure and edification.

If the artist is not a Christian, we are given the opportunity to come to grips with and better understand the needs and struggles of the unredeemed. We can only reach our world with the good news if we continually keep abreast of the questions non-Christians are asking and the ever-changing perspectives of the modern world.

If the artist is a Christian who is able to combine excellence of form with a content that reflects a Christian commitment, our worldview is expanded, refined, and sensitized. Often, the godly artist sees things about the church and the culture which surrounds it far more clearly than most of us, and is often truly prophetic in the exercise of that gift. Dostoevski saw much of the error of our culture as far back as the nineteenth century. Walker Percy was a twentieth-century writer who saw deeply into the ills of modern life and its moral collapse.

When our children are exposed to the best of the Christian tradition, it has a critical influence on how the Christian faith permeates their thinking, their feeling, and their ability to make moral choices. Too often our children only experience Christianity in the form of rules, dogmas, and rituals. As important as all these are, it is more important that Christianity influence deep down the way they see reality. A Christian vision will give them the courage to choose what is truly good and empower them to cope with love, discernment, and sympathy in a world lacking in moral virtue and emotional stability.

Finally, art can be an effective tool for sharing the gospel. Unfortunately, all too often, Christian artists let the content swamp the form and the message strangle the artfulness of the telling. But when done well, because of its indirect methods, art can bypass our defenses and smuggle the truth into our lives. Countless stories can be told of people who were set on the road toward truth by the disquieting work of a powerful novel, a well-crafted film, or even the austere and orderly beauty of a Bach concerto. Art can and does transform lives.

The Poverty of Modern Christian Art

Francis Schaeffer said that "the Christian is the one whose imagination should fly beyond the stars." Instead, much of our modern Christian art is mired in an unbiblical religiosity and never gets off the ground. The reasons for this are largely twofold.

First, we are too focused on purely religious themes. Many think that for art to be Christian it must be explicitly so. This limits art to a few religious themes and the retelling of Bible stories. But this viewpoint is too narrow. Even the Bible does not limit its stories to those which teach an obvious and explicitly religious theme. The Song of Solomon, for example, is more a celebration of marital love than it is a religious tract. Similarly, the temple was decorated with carvings of almond blossoms, which had no specifically religious connotation; they were carved there as a beautiful adornment. All of reality is under the Christian purview, and the Christian artist is free to explore all subjects from the perspective of the Christian faith. In creation, God pronounced that the material world was good. We deny this when we try to force art to always be spiritual. Whether implicit or explicit, the Christian artists' worldview will shine through in subtle ways even if the theme is not directly a religious one.

Second, we are too limited to realism in art. Many Christians feel that realism is the only appropriate art form for the believing artist and that abstraction is inappropriate. Once again, such a view is too narrow. Metaphors (hardly a literalistic literary form) are abundant throughout Scripture, and God's chosen art was sometimes abstract. The priests who entered into the Holy of Holies wore robes decorated with blue pomegranates. Any horticulturist will tell you that such a fruit does not exist anywhere in the created order! There are no such things as blue pomegranates.

The fundamental fault of much Christian art is that it is too didactic. For example, many Christian writers seem to feel obligated to, in the words of Christian literary critic Leland

Ryken, "spell it out." Instead of letting the story's truth naturally unfold, we try to force it to speak too explicitly. Now there is nothing wrong with a clear exposition of the gospel. It is indeed imperative to explain clearly and carefully. But a work of art is not the place to do it. Art that is too didactic loses its power as art. Ryken notes that "the method of art is to incarnate meaning in concrete form. The artist *shows,* and is never content only to *tell* in the form of propositions. The strategy of art is to enact rather than summarize."[4]

C. S. Lewis' *The Chronicles of Narnia* may be the most profound work of theology produced in modern times. This is not because it details the points of a systematic theology but because it gives us a vision for the greatness and the mercy of God. The power of these books is in their slow revelation of the truth. We are not bludgeoned with the message. The character of Aslan, the great lion, is never directly presented as a type of Christ. Instead, as we read, it slowly begins to dawn on us that this is one who is like Christ, as Christ might have appeared in another context, namely in Narnia. The power of this work of art comes at least partially from the fact that the truth sneaks up on us and allows us to discover it for ourselves.

A steady diet of second-rate Christian art will do your children no more spiritual good than much that is crassly secular. In fact, it might do real harm because it can inoculate them against the power of real art and satisfy their tastes with the less-than-excellent. We must get beyond using art for purposes of utilitarian persuasion.

In the past, when the church was less concerned about the utilitarian propaganda value of art and more interested in the quality and craftsmanship, the church had a far greater influence on society. It worked deep down at the most basic level of presuppositions and actually affected the way people thought and the attitudes they held. C. S. Lewis wrote, "What we want is not more little books about Christianity, but more little books by Christians on other subjects—with their Christianity latent."

How Do We Judge a Work of Art?

I believe that only art of quality is worth our time and effort. Only fine art offers us lasting pleasure and real enlightenment. But how do we discover truly fine art?

It's important that we learn how to judge a work of art. I'd like to suggest some criteria which may help you:

1. *Technical excellence.* Is this a work which evidences careful craftsmanship, is worth repeated listenings, viewings, and readings, and makes full use of its chosen medium? Or is it slapdash, shallow, and propagandistic? The best art is often not fully graspable by a cursory exposure. We have to spend time with it.

2. *Intellectual content.* Does this work, whether Christian or non-Christian, speak the truth about reality? While we do not expect it to illumine every facet of truth, is it true in its picture of reality? Francis Schaeffer said that there were two great themes in art. The major theme is the ultimate meaningfulness of life, the beauty of creation, and the joy of relationship with God. The minor theme is man's fallenness and the devastation this brings to the created order. Therefore the despairing vision of Kafka and Arthur Miller's *Death of a Salesman* tell the truth, even if it is not the whole truth. A balanced diet of reading will include books which express both of these themes. A few pinnacles of artistry, like Dostoevski's *The Brothers Karamazov*, balance both themes with grace and power. An important element in understanding a work is to try to come to grips with its worldview.

3. *Integration of content and artistic medium.* Does the message fit the artistic garb in which it is enclosed? T. S. Eliot's fragmented poem "The Wasteland" is an illustration of the fragmented and fallen world in which we live and an example of message and medium complementing each other. But sometimes they do not. We must ask ourselves whether, for example, some of today's cheap and tawdry popular music can be used effectively to present the message of spiritual

truth. Or does such music only give us a feeling of warm fuzziness and a shallow and subjective emotional workout? I am not, of course, saying that such music has no value, but only suggesting that we be discerning about what we take into our minds and hearts.

Art can truly be a source of meaning, genuine pleasure, and enlightenment. We must find ways to bring the treasures of the world of art before our children's eyes so that they might have a deeper, more humane, and more spiritually powerful vision of their world. If we ourselves have grown up without these riches, it is never too late to learn to appreciate them.

Resources and Suggestions for Making Art a Part of Your Children's Lives

Things to Do

VISIT A MUSEUM

When it comes to great art, there is no substitute for seeing the real thing. As soon as your children are old enough, arrange a trip to the closest available art museum. Prepare in advance by researching one or two of the artists whose work is prominently featured. Study their lives and look at some pictures of their work. Children enjoy seeing in "real life" a picture which they know from a book of art prints. Keep the preparation light, and then resist the tendency to turn the visit into a minilecture. That is the quickest way to ruin the experience for your kids and, consequently, for you too. Simply enjoy and experience the beauty.

Then, when you get home, ask your children which works they liked best and why. Talk about works that were hard to understand. Compare the different styles and periods, asking yourself why certain artists choose to approach their work in the way they do.

FILL YOUR HOME WITH ART

In times past, only the rich could afford to adorn their homes with masterpieces of art. Now, in modern times, art reproductions and posters are widely available. It used to be that only one person could hang Van Gogh's "Starry Night" on his wall because there was only one copy in existence and the price was out of the reach of even many of the rich. Now we can all fill our homes with beautiful pictures and draw from them the rich contemplation which comes as a result of living day in and day out with a great masterpiece. Of course, the reproduction is never as good as the real thing (that's why visiting galleries is so important), but it is certainly a reasonable approximation!

Our family has a number of reproductions which we have permanently displayed in different parts of our house. We know one family who displays pictures in a particular area on the mantel. Every two or three weeks they put up a different picture by a different artist. This provides a lesson in art history for both parents and kids, and helps broaden everyone's appreciation for art.

If you have the resources, don't limit yourself to reproductions. Buy some fine original paintings or sculptures for your home. Many artists are struggling to make a living and could use your support. And who knows, any of them might be the next Rembrandt or Picasso!

CREATE YOUR OWN MASTERPIECES

Another way to own original works of art is to create them yourself. Perhaps some lessons and a little practice will reveal previously unknown talent in someone in your family.

Always keep plenty of paper, pencils, paste, and paints around. Give your kids a "legal" place to make a mess and let them have at it. Occasionally you can give them assignments to paint certain things (a still life, for example). It's always a joy to display work created by a loved one.

Books to Read

Sometimes, our own relative ignorance of art and art history keeps us from passing much knowledge in this area down to our kids. This is, however, a limitation anyone can overcome with a minimal amount of time expenditure. There are a number of books which will give you a helpful overview of art history, and will do a great deal to orient you to the world of art.

H. W. Janson's *History of Art* is a classic in this field. But if its price and bulk scare you away, try his excellent book (co-written with Anthony Janson) *History of Art for Young People*. It is clearly written, well-illustrated, and affordably priced, and includes a bibliography for more detailed study.

Perhaps my favorite is E. M. Gombrich's *The Story of Art*. A wonderful selection of prints, a readable text, and its availability in paperback make it an excellent choice.

Once you have familiarized yourself with art history, you might want to explore what some Christian writers have published on this subject. Gene Veith, Jr.'s *State of the Arts* not only gives a powerful biblical justification of the arts, but also includes a lengthy section that reflects on art history from a Christian perspective. Entitled "A Walk Through the Museum," this chapter will help you wed an appreciation for the arts with a real sense of biblical discernment.

Hans Rookmaker's *Modern Art and the Death of a Culture* examines the difference between the worldview of the modern and the worldview of the classic artist. Rookmaker shows how vulgar and ugly art is a reflection of the spiritual poverty of our culture as a whole. Also valuable is Rookmaker's *Art Needs No Justification* (mentioned earlier in this chapter).

Francis Schaeffer's *How Should We Then Live?* attempts to connect the development of the arts with other cultural developments since the Renaissance. Though it is by no means exhaustive, it does shed light on the way in which art reflects the worldview of its times.

Stock your home library with books which feature numerous reproductions of famous paintings. It is easy to spend a small fortune collecting books like these (Abrams publishes some especially fine but very pricey volumes), but you don't need to. Your local bookstore probably has a sale table with many such volumes on it.

Once you have purchased some of these volumes, make them available to your kids. Don't buy books that are so expensive you have to constantly worry about the children ruining them. Let your children spend time leafing through them, simply enjoying the pictures without interference from Mom and Dad. My youngest daughter, Kathryn, spends delighted hours poring over some of our many art books, just slowly turning the pages and enjoying the artwork.

An affordable and informative series of paperback art books is published by Thames and Hudson. This series contains volumes on nearly every major artist and school of art. They are written by experts but are understandable to the intelligent nonexpert. Once you discover artists whom you particularly enjoy, the appropriate book on that artist will provide you with biographical information and attractive (though small) reproductions of their work.

For the young reader, Children's Press has published an excellent series of biographies of famous artists by Mike Venezia called *Getting to Know the World's Great Artists*. This series is distinguished by its impish humor, quality reproductions of famous paintings, and a reasonable price. A third grader can easily read these books, but they are interesting enough that adults will gain from them as well. At about 32 pages each, you can read them in a single sitting. Artists currently available in the series include: Botticelli, Pieter Bruegel, Mary Cassatt, Da Vinci, Salvador Dali, Paul Gauguin, Francisco Goya, Edward Hopper, Paul Klee, Michelangelo, Monet, Georgia O'Keeffe, Picasso, Jackson Pollock, Rembrandt, and Van Gogh.

Take some time soon in your local bookstore to explore the art section and make an investment in the growth of your children's appreciation for the arts.

Music has charms to soothe a savage
  breast,
To soften rocks, or bend a knotted oak.
I've heard that things inanimate have
  moved,
And, as with living souls, have been
  informed
By magic numbers and pervasive sound.
                                    —Congreve

Next to theology I give music the highest
  place of honor.
                                    —Martin Luther

•   •   •

15

Music to Calm the Savage Breast

Music and the Growth of the Soul

*M*usic is all around us. You cannot go anywhere without hearing some sort of music playing away in the background. The recording industry has become a multi-billion-dollar industry with some of the most popular artists selling millions of copies of their records.

Once, we had to stay stationary to listen to music. Now, in the form of boom boxes and walkmans, we can take our music with us. And millions do. Especially teenagers. They listen while in the car, while they party, and while they study. Few are the hours that the music is not plugged in and playing loud. And the music of preference is usually rock.

How much time do our young people spend listening to music? According to studies, between the seventh and twelfth grades the average teenager listens to 10,500 hours of rock music—just slightly less than the entire number of hours spent in the classroom from kindergarten through high school. Considering this startling statistic, maybe we should examine whether this is time well spent and explore alternatives with our children during these formative years of their developing taste.

The Power of Music

What is it about music that is so powerful? After all, it is only the noise made when stretched gut is drawn across a taut string; it is only the sound that results from blowing into a tube; it is only the beating of a small hammer against metal wires. This is one way to explain playing a violin, a flute, or a piano. And yet, when an accomplished musician takes one of these instruments in hand, music is produced which can quiet or stir our hearts, move us to powerful emotions, cause relaxation, or incite tension. The power in music can't be explained by physics alone. Somehow music touches us deeply.

The mystery of music's impact defies explanation or analysis. We only grope in the dark to find the reasons behind its power. Music as an art form grips us in a different way than books or paintings. Its message cannot be transferred into words or pictures. It somehow strikes us more directly. This is what the philosopher Schopenhauer was saying when he wrote this about the nature of music:

> Music . . . stands quite alone. It is cut off from all the other arts. . . . It does not express a particular and definite joy, sorrow, anguish, horror, delight, or mood of peace, but joy, sorrow, anguish, horror, delight, peace of mind themselves, in the abstract, in their essential nature, without accessories, and therefore without their customary motives. Yet it enables us to grasp and share them fully in this quintessence.[1]

This is both the power and the danger of music. Someone once said, "Let me write the songs of a nation and I do not care who writes its laws." The thought behind this comment is that music has a powerful ability to affect our values and our character. After Handel's first London performance of *Messiah*, Lord Kinnoul congratulated him on his excellent "entertainment." Handel replied, "My Lord, I should be sorry if I only entertain them. I wish to make them better."

Plato recognized this long ago. In his book *The Republic*, he draws up the outline for an ideal society. It is striking that in a book on the ideal society Plato gives only two pages to the discussion of economics, but a full 40 pages to the type of music its citizens should listen to and how musical training for the young should be undertaken. For Plato, music was not just an afterthought in education, but one of the critical elements in teaching children about virtuous living.

> Musical training is a more potent instrument than any other, because rhythm and harmony find their way into the inward places of the soul, on which they mightily fasten, imparting grace.[2]

Plato believed that music was a concrete expression of the order or disorder in the human soul. In other words, that music reflected the state of the soul of the one who played or listened to it. If the soul was at harmony with itself and with the gods, then the music would be a reflection of this. If the soul was in turmoil, this too would show itself forth in the music. A contemporary rock band gained immense popularity recently with its brooding, dark sound and despairing and cynical lyrics. At the crest of their popularity, the lead vocalist of this band, a young man with all the riches and possessions any person could want, put the business end of a shotgun to his head and pulled the trigger. Certainly, this was a tragic waste of a young life, but it should have come as no surprise to his fans. The vision of disharmony and despair was obvious in the music his band produced.

The Greeks were so moved by music that they ascribed it to the gods, the "Muses." In fact, many ancient and medieval thinkers felt that music was part of the nature of the universe itself. The doctrine they taught was the "music of the spheres." Each planet was believed to produce a certain note. When these were heard together they produced a harmonious and glorious sound. Two modern Christian writers have carried forward the idea of the creative power of music. In C. S. Lewis' *The Magician's Nephew* (the sixth installment in the *Chronicles of Narnia*), Aslan creates the universe by singing it into existence. In the first chapter of J. R. R. Tolkien's *The Silmarillion*, music is the creative force that brings Middle Earth into existence.

If it is true that music has this kind of awesome force, we must ask ourselves whether certain kinds of music are better than others, more spiritually positive in their effect, perhaps. Some disagree with the idea that music can be morally bad, but listen to what Peter Kreeft says in his book *Making Choices*:

> Is there such a thing as morally good and bad music? That would make no sense at all if morality were only about justice and rights and duties, as it is in most modern discussion. But if morality is about the alignment or misalignment of our whole being with the goodness of God, then anything that touches or moves our whole being is morally relevant. And music certainly does that.[3]

And so we need to examine carefully the place of music in our lives.

Music and Silence

Sometimes the best music is no music at all. Silence is sometimes the most pleasant of sounds.

What is it we fear that we keep ourselves bombarded with sound all our waking hours? Why do we so avoid silence in conversation or the quiet that settles over a room as the sun goes down, its last lazy rays retreating across the floor?

The place of silence in our lives is the place of healing and re-creation. The silence quiets our hearts and gives us pause for reflection. In silence we come face to face with ourselves, in all our frailty and sinfulness. Silence prepares us for change in that it allows us to hear the voice of God deep within our hearts. Finally, silence brings peace and contentment, and gives us room to gain true perspective on our lives. In moments of silence we are flooded with those things that really count. As adults we know we need these advantages of silence. But our children desperately need them too. The child is already so driven by the forward thrust of adrenaline that it is difficult to find a place of quiet and calm.

In a natural and unforced way we need to marshal the natural moments of silence during each day. When silence falls, resist the tendency to reach for the knob on the radio or record player. Silence is golden, a precious treasure we should cultivate in our lives. Let silence flood your home from time to time, and you will find that peace will follow in its wake.

When you do turn on music in your home, let it be music of beauty and substance.

The Importance of Good Music

Good music sets an atmosphere within our homes. It reflects something of what we value and treasure. Just as the background music in a film reflects the mood of the scene we are viewing, so the music we choose to play in our home will reflect the mood of our home. Whether it's the adrenaline surge of up-tempo music, the lazy contemplation of jazz, or the soothing calm of a classical piece, music helps set the atmosphere in our home.

Relaxing music has a calming effect on the environment in the home. Remember the biblical account of King Saul's need for the soothing effects of music. He was tormented by an evil spirit. But when David played his harp, "relief would come to Saul; he would feel better, and the evil spirit would leave him" (1 Samuel 16:23). Some medical studies indicate that music lessens our physiological reactions to stress by increasing the release of endorphins, our natural pain relievers. Other studies claim that music helps to speed healing and reduce the danger of infection. Cheri Fuller, in her book *How to Grow a Young Music Lover,* tells the story of a friend who was severely, almost suicidally, depressed. Nothing, including prayer and Bible reading, could bring her out of this state. What finally caused her to emerge from this deep despair was music. When she began to sing songs and hymns, she felt the cloud of depression lift.

The music of praise is such a powerful ally in our struggle against the evil one. In 2 Chronicles 20 God instructed Jehoshaphat to send singers out in front of the army. Praising the beauty of God's holiness, they set the stage for a miracle. In their confusion, the enemies of Israel began to slaughter each other, and Jehoshaphat's army carried the day. Remember also the three young Hebrews—Shadrach, Meshach and Abednego—who sang praises to God in the midst of the fiery furnace and were preserved from harm. Music of praise to God is a powerful thing!

Beautiful music can create in your home the kind of atmosphere where peace and joy reign. But what if your child chooses to play music which you find offensive and non-conducive to the atmosphere of your home? In many homes the battle line drawn over music results in a souring of parent-child relationships. Maintaining musical control is rarely worth alienating your child. Instead, try a more creative method of influence. Rather than simply laying down the law, take the time to try to understand your child's music. In so doing, you might uncover issues and problems which gentle love can heal and mend. You might want to try sitting down with your son or daughter and listening together to the objectionable songs. You can then discuss what the singer is trying to say and analyze it in terms of your family's values. Open, rational discussion goes a lot further than rigid rejection.

While I was in my latter years of high school I fell in for the first time with a more popular crowd. These were the kids whose friendship and company were prized by everyone in the school. I started listening to their music. One of the "in group's" favorite singers was a rocker whose music spilled forth in driving bass and drum rhythms and wailing, plaintive guitar solos. But his songs were characterized by crude and obscene lyrics. I managed to ignore this until the day I was playing the tape loudly in my room and my mother walked in. She sat down and listened to a couple of songs with me and made one pertinent comment. Without anger or judgment she simply said in response to the song we had just heard, "You know, that's really a sick thing to say." I flushed with embarrassment as I realized how really raunchy the song was. I had ignored the message because I liked the music, but the vileness of it struck me for the first time so strongly that I got rid of the tape. No moral lecture had accomplished this—only the willingness of my mother to listen. My own conscience brought the conviction.

Music is a constantly recurring theme in the Scriptures. God loves music because, whether sung or played, it is an outpouring of our deepest emotions. Over 200 specific references in Scripture direct us to sing or make music unto the Lord. Music touches us deeply and it also touches the heart of God. So important is it that David puts it forth in the imperative:

> Shout for joy to the LORD, all the earth,
>> burst into jubilant song with music;
> make music to the LORD with the harp,
>> with the harp and the sound of singing,
> with trumpets and the blast of the ram's horn—
>> shout for joy before the LORD, the King
>> (Psalm 98:4-6).

> Praise the LORD.
> Praise God in his sanctuary;
>> praise him in his mighty heavens.
> Praise him for his acts of power;
>> praise him for his surpassing greatness.
> Praise him with the sounding of the trumpet,
>> praise him with the harp and lyre,

> praise him with tambourine and dancing,
>> praise him with the strings and flute,
> praise him with the clash of cymbals,
>> praise him with resounding cymbals.
> Let everything that has breath praise the LORD.
>> Praise the LORD (Psalm 150).

We learn from Revelation 5 that praise will be one of our primary occupations in heaven. Why not tune up our voice now?

Let us then strive to fill our homes with music of praise and music of great beauty. The rich heritage of music appreciation is much more than just a sort of cultural elitism. It builds order and beauty into the lives of our children and gives them a positive outlet for strong emotional feelings.

Francis Schaeffer tells the story of how as a young boy a chance hearing of Tchaikovsky's "1812 Overture" became the doorway that opened to him a whole new world of beauty. For me, it was Bach; I count my first listening to his "St. Matthew's Passion" as one of those rare and deeply enriching spiritual experiences that I will always treasure.

Introducing Your Children to Good Music

If music is such an important element in our spiritual lives, we must introduce our children to music that will have a powerfully uplifting effect on them. I happen to believe classical music can accomplish this. I am using the term "classical music" in its broadest sense, to mean orchestral and instrumental music produced from the time of the Renaissance onward.

I am not saying that classical music is the only good kind of music or that other kinds of music are necessarily bad in themselves. In fact, I have a deep appreciation for certain rock, jazz, folk, and country artists. I am a big fan of Bruce Cockburn, Mark Heard, Louis Armstrong, and Van Morrison. However, as much as I appreciate other kinds of music, there seems to be something special about much classical music. Its sophistication allows us to give it repeated listenings, always discovering something new. We are required to exercise patience and concentration to fully appreciate some of the more complex pieces. Its emphasis is on harmony and melody, providing a more relaxing, harmonious listening experience.

I have created a couple of lists to help you get started in your listening adventure. The first is a number of pieces that are more familiar and less demanding—what some call the "light classics." They all have catchy melodies both you and your children will appreciate. The second is a list of 100 works universally acknowledged as truly great masterpieces of music.

Getting Started: A List of "Light Classics"

I recommend the following list of classical pieces for their immediate accessibility, their entertainment value, and their appropriateness for the younger listener. Once your child develops a taste for these more "flashy" works, you can use the longer list that follows to begin listening to works demanding more effort and concentration. Remember to make the process fun. Don't tie your child to a chair and try to force-feed "culture." That will work against your intentions.

Benjamin Britten—A Young Person's Guide to the Orchestra
Sergei Prokofiev—Peter and the Wolf
George Gershwin—Rhapsody in Blue; An American in Paris
Aaron Copland—Rodeo; Billy the Kid
Peter Tchaikovsky—The Nutcracker; 1812 Overture
Johann Strauss, Jr.—Waltzes
Camille Saint-Saëns—Carnival of the Animals
Nikolai Rimsky-Korsakov—Scheherazade
Ralph Vaughn Williams—Fantasia on Greensleeves
Amilicare Ponchinelle—Dance of the Hours
Gustav Holst—The Planets

Suggestion: You might want to rent or purchase the Walt Disney film *Fantasia* as an introduction to classical music. Kids love it, though they may find some sections a bit frightening.

The following is a more advanced list and contains an abundance of fine music you'll want to expose yourself and your children to.

A Classical Music Beginner's List

The following list will get you started in your exploration of some of the world's most beautiful music. I've listed 100 pieces from which you can begin your classical music library.

Heinrich Schütz (1585-1672)
 Psalms of David

Johann Pachelbel (1653-1706)
 Canon

Antonio Vivaldi (1675-1741)
 Gloria in D
 The Four Seasons

Johann Sebastian Bach (1685-1750)
 St. Matthew Passion
 Magnificat in D
 Brandenburg Concertos
 Chaconne

George Freidrich Handel (1685-1759)
 Messiah
 Water Music

Franz Joseph Haydn (1732-1809)
 Symphony #94 in G (Surprise)
 Symphony #101 (Clock)
 Symphony #104 (London)

Wolfgang Amadeus Mozart (1756-1791)
 Requiem
 Symphony #39
 Symphony #40

Symphony #41 (Jupiter)
Piano Concerto #21 in C
Piano Concerto #20
Eine Kleine Nachtmusik

Ludwig Van Beethoven (1770-1827)
Symphony #3 (Eroica)
Symphony #5
Symphony #6 (Pastoral)
Symphony #7
Symphony #9 (Choral)
Piano Concerto #5 (Emporer)
Concerto in D for Violin
Piano Sonata #14 (Moonlight)
Piano Sonata #8 (Pathetique)

Franz Schubert (1797-1828)
Symphony #8 (Unfinished)
Symphony #9
Trout Quintet

Hector Berlioz (1803-1869)
Symphony Fantastique

Felix Mendelssohn (1809-1847)
Symphony #3 (Scotch)
Symphony #4 (Italian)
Symphony #5 (Reformation)
Violin Concerto in E
Midsummer Night's Dream

Frederic Chopin (1810-1849)
Piano Concerto #2
Waltzes
Polonaises

Franz Liszt (1811-1886)
Hungarian Rhapsodies
Piano Concerto #1

Richard Wagner (1813-1883)
Ring of the Nibelungen (highlights)

Johann Strauss, Jr. (1825-1899)
Waltzes

Johannes Brahms (1833-1897)
 Piano Concerto #1
 Piano Concerto #2
 Violin Concerto in D

Camille Saint-Saëns (1835-1921)
 Symphony #3 (Organ)
 Carnival of the Animals

Georges Bizet (1838-1875)
 Carmen

Modest Mussorgsky (1839-1881)
 Night on Bald Mountain
 Pictures From an Exhibition

Peter Ilyich Tchaikovsky (1840-1893)
 Symphony #6 (Pathetique)
 Swan Lake
 Sleeping Beauty
 The Nutcracker Suite
 Piano Concerto #1
 Concerto in D major for Violin
 Serenade for Strings
 1812 Overture

Antonin Dvorak (1841-1903)
 Symphony #9 (New World)
 Concerto in B minor for Cello

Eduard Grieg (1843-1907)
 Peer Gynt Suite
 Piano Concerto in A

Nikolai Rimsky-Korsakov (1844-1908)
 Scheherazade

Gustav Mahler (1860-1911)
 Symphony #1
 Symphony #2 (Resurrection)
 Symphony #4
 Symphony #9

Claude Debussy (1862-1918)
 Prelude to Afternoon of a Faun
 La Mer

Richard Strauss (1864-1949)
Don Juan
Till Eulenspiegel
Also Sprach Zarathustra

Jean Sibelius (1865-1957)
Finlandia
Symphony #1
Symphony #2
Symphony #5

Ralph Vaughn Williams (1872-1958)
Fantasia on Greensleeves

Sergei Rachmaninoff (1873-1943)
Piano Concerto #2
Piano Concerto #3

Gustav Holst (1874-1934)
The Planets

Arnold Schoenberg (1874-1951)
Five Orchestral Pieces

Maurice Ravel (1875-1937)
Bolero
Daphnis & Chloe

Igor Stravinsky (1882-1971)
Petrushka
The Rite of Spring

Sergei Prokofiev (1891-1953)
Peter and the Wolf
Symphony #5

George Gershwin (1898-1937)
American in Paris
Rhapsody in Blue
Concerto in F major

Aaron Copland (1900-1990)
Billy the Kid
Rodeo
Appalachian Spring

Dmitri Shostakovich (1906-1975)
   Symphony #1
   Symphony #5

Samuel Barber (1910-1981)
   Adagio for Strings

That's 99 pieces of classical music. I left one blank spot for your favorite piece of music. Before you invest your money in a particular cassette or CD, you might try checking it out from the library to see if you like it. When you do discover a composer you really enjoy, go ahead and explore beyond the few pieces listed here.

Building Your Classical Music Library

Building a classical music library doesn't necessarily mean spending a lot of money. You can often get high-quality performances at reasonable prices. Be aware, though, that some budget brands of classical recordings are sometimes recorded poorly or are sub-par renditions by unknown orchestras. A recording's poor quality can adversely affect your enjoyment of a piece of music. So stick with better brand names and well-known orchestras and conductors. Let a knowledgeable sales clerk at your local record store point you to the better budget labels. The Seraphim Budget classics and the Columbia "Great Performances" series are two of these.

Helpful Resources on Classical Music

The following list of books will help you expand your knowledge and understanding of classical music:

Leonard Bernstein, *The Joy of Music*, New York: Simon
   and Schuster, 1959.
   *This classic introduction to the art of listening is one
   of the best.*

Aaron Copland, *What to Listen For in Music*, rev. ed.,
   New York: McGraw-Hill, 1957.
   The great modern composer writes for the beginner.

Mary Ann Froehlich, *Music Education in the Christian Home*, Brentwood, TN: Wolgemuth and Hyatt, 1990.
Especially valuable for parents who want their children to play a musical instrument and learn music theory.

Cheryl Fuller, *How to Grow a Young Music Lover*, Wheaton, IL: Harold Shaw, 1994.
This book is extremely practical and filled with useful things you can do to build the love of music into your child. It has a wonderful section on ways to introduce your children to the great composers.

M. Goffstein, *A Little Schubert*, New York: Harper and Row, 1985.
A delightful picture book which celebrates the joy of music.

Donald J. Grout, *A History of Western Music*, rev. ed., New York: Norton, 1973.
The standard history of music, this book will tell you everything you need to know about music history.

Patrick Kavanaugh, *The Spiritual Lives of the Great Composers*, Nashville: Sparrow, 1992.
Short biographies of several composers, emphasizing their spiritual commitments. Some interesting material.

Patrick Kavanaugh, *A Taste for the Classics*, Nashville: Sparrow, 1993.
A guide for the person who wants to seriously explore the world of classical music. Includes listening guides to lead you through your own personal study and listening experience.

Joseph Machlis, *The Enjoyment of Music*, 3rd ed., New York: Norton, 1970.
A good introduction which contains valuable material on the lives of the composers.

Simon Mundy, *The Usborne Story of Music*, London: Usborne, 1980.

A short and simple overview for the beginner. Especially good for children as it is heavily illustrated.

Jane S. Smith and Betty Carlson, *The Gift of Music: Great Composers and Their Influence*, Westchester, IL: Crossway Books, 1987.
This book emphasizes the composers' relationship to the Christian faith and is rich in anecdotal material.

*Only the passions, only great passions,
can elevate the mind to great things.*
—Denis Diderot

*To burn always with this hard, gemlike
flame, to maintain this ecstasy, is success in
life.*

—Walter Pater

•   •   •

16

Taking Fun Seriously

Leisure, Sports, and Passion

$\mathcal{T}$he well-rounded child is not only intellectually and spiritually strong, but also physically strong. Scripture teaches that the body is the "temple of the Holy Spirit" (1 Corinthians 6:19), the dwelling place of God's Spirit. But our bodies are more than just "containers." We are not bodiless phantoms; God has made us creatures of flesh and blood. Some Christians today make the same mistake as the Gnostics of old, believing that the body is somehow evil. But God Himself took on human flesh in the person of Jesus Christ, and redeemed us from the consequences of the fall. God entered into the world of flesh and showed us how, while still in the flesh, we can begin to live out the eternal life He has promised to us. It is left to us to receive His gift of grace and to walk in communion with Him during our earthly pilgrimage.

We can learn to enjoy our life in the body, not merely mark time while we wait for our new home in heaven. We can begin to enjoy heaven now. We can learn to joy in the gifts God has given us—our awesome body, which functions with a complexity surpassing any machine; the glories and the majesty of the physical world; the wonder and mystery of human love and romance; the thrill of creative achievement; the warmth and comfort of family and friends. "Carpe diem"—we should seize the days here on earth and live life to its fullest, with passion and intensity. Let us never have our eyes so fixed on heaven that we miss the rich banquet of gifts to which God calls us in this life below.

The reason many people reject Christianity is because they have intellectual problems with it—these objections can most often be answered decisively. They reject the Christian faith because it seems to offer a shallow, sterile vision of human life. They look at those who proclaim the name of Jesus and see rigidity, narrowness, and lack of passion. In his poem "The Second Coming," William Butler Yeats captures the truth about our modern times: We lack the strong conviction of our beliefs.

> Things fall apart; the center cannot hold;
> Mere anarchy is loosed upon the world,
> The blood-dimmed tide is loosed, and everywhere
> The ceremony of innocence is drowned;
> The best lack all conviction, while the worst
> Are full of passionate intensity.

When we see the world through God's eyes, we see that even though the darkness attempts to stifle the beauty and goodness of life, the mark of the Creator is always evident.

Leisure and the Sabbath Principle

To discover the true joy of existence, to let the harmony of creation sing along our bones and burrow deep within our heart—tunneling past our hurts and pains—is to know the principle of Sabbath. After expending six days of labor to create the world, God rested on the seventh day, and He called this day of rest "holy." On this seventh day God looked over His creation, pondering what He had created, and He pronounced it "good." This was a day of leisure, a day for rest, a day for contemplating what He had done.

We too need times of Sabbath, times when the rush of accomplishment gives way to thankfulness for what God has done in our lives. We need those times when our inner resources can be reinvigorated, our batteries recharged. In our culture, many do not understand the divine rhythm of Sabbath, where accomplishment is followed by leisure. Many of us are overachievers. Recent studies show that people in the business world are working increasingly longer hours, sometimes as many as seven days a week. Then, when they do get a chance to rest and recuperate, their inner resources are so depleted that their leisure is frittered away in laziness, rather than true restfulness. True Sabbath is not just a cessation of activity, but a quieting of the heart.

The peace of God comes to us when we quiet our hearts, our minds, and our ambitions. I treasure the times when I can simply sit and "think along with God." If the sun is shining, I'll grab a glass of iced tea and sit outside. If it's cold or raining, my favorite armchair will do. I allow myself the luxury of just sitting and thinking. I experience Sabbath during these times as I assimilate what's going on in my life—in my job, in my character growth (or lack of it), in my spiritual life. I let my mind wander over new things I have learned, new experiences I have had, new ideas I have received from friends and colleagues. I always end in prayer, but because of the pondering that has preceded it, it is prayer that is focused, heartfelt, and passionate. I find it is only as I make space in my schedule for such times of "doing nothing" that I can keep perspective in my life and not get caught up in the rush of the momentary and the expedient. If our children can learn the value of Sabbath leisure, they will discover a way to live before God in relevance and depth. This form of "doing nothing" accomplishes more than all our straining after achievement.

Of course, all our leisure does not have to consist of quiet reflection. There is definitely a place for fun in our lives. Our God is a God of laughter and humor. A glance at the parables reveals that Jesus had a lively sense of ironic humor. The picture He gives us of His kingdom is that of a wedding feast—a rollicking, freewheeling, ongoing party! So beware of being more serious and straight-laced than our Master Himself. Some Christians mistake legalism for holiness. Holiness is not a form of self-denial as much as it is a setting apart for God's purposes. Even our times of fun and laughter can be holy in that they are set aside for God. We can learn a lot from our leisure activities. Let's look at sports to see how athletic involvement can be a positive moral force in the lives of our kids.

Moral Values in Sports

I am an avid (though not very good) golfer. But the time I spend on the golf course is not only physically invigorating, it also helps clear my mind of the clutter of responsibilities and allows me to step back and get a renewed picture of life. Similarly, I enjoy a game of one-on-one basketball or shooting hoops.

As well as exercising and strengthening the body, athletics can teach us many valuable moral lessons.

1. *Sports teach us to cooperate.* Team sports, which emphasize working together to achieve a common goal (a basket, a touchdown, a goal), provide us with a picture of how we must all work together to achieve anything of value. We learn to utilize one another's unique abilities, sometimes letting personal desires and plans fall to the side so that the team may function more smoothly. Of course, this is what we do in life. As John Donne has written, "No man is an island."

2. *Sports teach us to lose gracefully.* In sports, as in life, we do not always win. Sometimes things fail to go our way and others triumph over us. When this happens, and we are left

with the stigma of being second best (it happens to everyone in some area eventually!), we are presented with an opportunity to learn how to lose gracefully, accepting that this time some-one else has done better than we have. To learn to accept this without bitterness or grudging is to learn an important moral value which can help us in all of life.

3. *Sports teach us to win gracefully.* Sometimes we actu-ally do come out on top. Just as we need to learn to accept defeat, we can also learn to be humble in victory. When we understand the truth about real priorities in life, we can resist the tendency to arrogantly crow over our victories. Winning and losing are both less important than playing the game with integrity and having fun doing it.

4. *Sports teach us about fairness.* In any sporting compe-tition, each participant must abide by the rules agreed upon. Cheating may steal the game, but it also steals away the true victory. As in sport, so in life. If we do not play fairly, there is no value in the game. When we cheat another, we find that we really cheat ourselves.

5. *Sports teach us about individual talents and limita-tions.* Not everybody can do everything equally well. Every-one is worthy of equal respect, but we are not all created equal in terms of our gifts and abilities. Maturity is not only recog-nizing your strengths, but also admitting your weaknesses. Part of knowing ourselves is knowing our limitations.

6. *Sports teach us to respect our bodies.* Our physical body is a precious gift from God. Our bodies need exercise, proper nutrition, and freedom from intoxicants and pollutants (such as drugs) which would desecrate the temple of God by weakening it. Our bodies are so intimately connected with our emotional well-being that poor health or physical exhaustion can be enough to cause depression.

7. *Sports teach us about discipline.* Only through disci-pline, practice, and hard work does true mastery of a skill become reality. If we can discipline ourselves, we can excel at our chosen athletic endeavor and find true excellence. Disci-pline is the key that unlocks real growth in our spiritual lives,

in our character development, and in our moral victory over unruly passions.

Finally, sports provide fun and enjoyment in our lives. They are one way that we can "seize the day!" The famous runner, Eric Liddell, whose story is immortalized in the film *Chariots of Fire*, once spoke of his exultation whenever he participated in his chosen sport of running: "When I run," he said, "I feel His glory." Sports can make us feel good about ourselves and clear our focus in life. A passion for excellence in sport is not all that far from a passion for moral excellence. Both come as a result of concentrated effort, practice, and putting God's gifts to use.

Balanced Lives

Sports, leisure, and fun bring balance to our lives. All the intellectual, artistic, and spiritual pursuits discussed in the previous chapters need to be balanced with a focus on a healthy body. Our bodies, minds, and spirits are all interconnected. If we focus on the growth of one to the neglect of the other two, we will fail to be all that God created us to be. The Christian vision of life brings the lordship of Christ into every part of our lives.

We must exercise our minds and bodies. We must work to improve our bodily health as well as our spiritual health. We must learn when to laugh and when to be serious-minded. This kind of balance will bring about a full and rich life—one in which the passion to live life to the fullest will be wedded with the passion to please God.

People are generally better persuaded by the reasons which they have themselves discovered than by those which have come into the mind of others.

—Pascal

•   •   •

17

The Road
to Christian Adulthood

The Gift of a Moral Imagination

*T*here comes that moment when you look at your children and realize that childhood is something in the past. It doesn't happen overnight. It is a slow process of developing independence. But the day comes that they are ultimately responsible for their own lives, for their choices and decisions, and their direction in life. Someday all your parental efforts will come to a culminating juncture. We never stop being parents, of course, but our role changes dramatically. Still, even though it is a natural and inevitable moment, it can be frightening for parents.

It is a glorious thing to realize that the small babies you once cradled in your arms are now adult people. Though they still love and care for you, they are no longer dependent on you in the same way they once were. They are, in a very real sense, on their own. They may choose life partners. And this is as it should be. This is God's plan: "For this reason a man will leave his father and mother and be united to his wife . . ." (Genesis 2:24). Much of our effort as parents is in preparation for that day. If our children will be successful Christians in their own right, we must have bequeathed to them, by the way we have raised them, the gift of a moral vision. And if our children have caught the moral vision we have tried so hard to impart, the moment of leaving can be a moment of joy.

Our goal as parents is to set our children on a path to spiritual, emotional, and intellectual maturity. One day they will begin to navigate the difficulties of life without their former dependence upon you, and then they must choose either to walk the path alone or walk it with God.

We want our children to continue to grow and develop as people and as believers, and so somewhere along the way they must discover that learning is a lifetime pursuit. Now, if this is our attitude and one of our dearly cherished practices, they will learn this from us. All too often, graduation from formal schooling signals the end of learning. Studies reveal that the average U.S. college graduate reads on the average only one book per year! One cannot help but wonder if this is because these students consider themselves so "educated" that they already know everything they need to know. I cannot think of a more deadly attitude to continued personal growth. We must always stay open to learning new things and have the humility to recognize how little we really do know. Charles Spurgeon (echoing the words of Socrates) defined the truly wise like this:

> In the case of these wise men, we see ignorance admitted. The truly wise men are never above asking questions. . . . The knowledge of our ignorance is the doorstep to the temple of knowledge.[1]

The person who ceases to ask questions, ceases to learn. The person who ceases to learn, ceases to grow. This is true for spiritual growth as well as intellectual growth.

Through our actions, we can demonstrate to our children our own thirst for learning. We must spend rich time in the study of the Scriptures, read quality books (both modern and classic), research new areas of interest, and constantly stretch ourselves beyond the complacency that can so easily overtake us. Of course, we will never be perfect parents. Thank God that our children can rise above our parental inadequacies to become the kind of people God intends them to be.

Our ultimate goal is to raise children who become responsible, virtuous, intelligent adult believers, not unthinking carbon copies of our own beliefs and prejudices. Let us set our goals high.

The Challenge:
A Life of Passion, Wisdom,
Beauty, and Character

The true life of the Christian is much more than a set of beliefs to which a person gives assent. It is a daily process of transformation through the miracle of grace. From glory to glory we are transformed into His likeness and image, becoming new people, new creations of our loving heavenly Father. The challenge is to cooperate with the movements of grace by living passionately and wisely, manifesting both beauty and character.

To live passionately is to bring every part of our lives into the embrace of the gospel, to reach our true potential through finding God's plan and will for us, and to experience both pain and joy in all its fullness, trusting that God is Lord over all. It is easy to fritter our lives away in conformity and safety. If we are always careful to fit in and not rock the boat, if we are always looking to others to tell us what to think and how to feel, we rob ourselves of the joy of living in authenticity. Living by the Gospel often means going against the flow, subverting the shallow values of our culture, and refusing to accept the comfortable norms of our society. To live passionately is to do more than believe; it is enjoy God's gifts freely, to glory in the small things, and to pursue His truth with our whole being. To live passionately is to do more than believe; it is to *experience* our faith.

To live wisely is to seek the perspective of God, realizing the limits of our own finitude and searching out the design of the One who created us. To live wisely is to immerse our minds in the Word of God so that our prejudices, our preconceptions and our presuppositions might be challenged and our mind thereby transformed. To live wisely is to be teachable, to expose ourselves to men and women who have gone before us and reflected on the kinds of experiences common to us all. To live wisely is to have more than just an emotional attachment to our faith; it is to engage our minds and think it through.

To live a life of beauty is to see with renewed vision, below the surface of life into what the poet Gerard Manley Hopkins called "the dearest freshness deep down things." To live in beauty is to wonder at the marvelous works of God and the mirror of His work in human creativity. To live in beauty is to seek for the very best, never satisfied with the shallow, the tawdry, the empty, and the false. Our fallen world is so marked by the damage of human sin that bringing beauty into the lives of others gives them hope and points them toward the truth. To live in beauty is to appreciate what God has done through others, and to attempt to make the world just a little more livable by glorying in the creative gifts He has given us. To live in beauty means to resist dullness and conformity and to find the lovely and important in our life and faith.

Finally, to manifest character is to be a picture of Jesus Christ—a living, breathing example of His holiness and love. "By their fruits you will recognize them," said Jesus (Matthew 7:16). We must learn to make choices which honor God and His moral law, practicing the moral virtues and living in such a way that others capture a glimpse of God's love, mercy, and righteousness in the way we conduct ourselves. To manifest character is to practice integrity in our dealings with others, show respect for their uniqueness, and extend long-suffering forgiveness when they bring hurt or pain into our lives.

The power of this kind of life is that people are drawn to it. It is a life that will help your children ignore the false glamour of the world's temptations and strengthen every part of their being: their mind, their emotions, their body, and their spirit. Jesus lived this kind of life. People were drawn to Him because they saw the difference between their lives and His.

Our world lies under the powerful influence of many false gods. Gods of materialism, ideology, paganism, violence, the media, unbridled sexuality, and unbalanced trust in the power of reason. These gods will devour our children if we do not model a better way. And though these lesser gods are not without power and influence, they will find themselves unable to overpower the children of a greater God—the God who revealed Himself in Jesus Christ.

May our children see God and themselves more clearly, and with that insight work to make the world a better place for their fellow men and women.

May their imaginations be fired by the glorious vision of that which is truly good, beautiful, important, and true.

May they live lives that manifest high moral virtue and the character manifest in the righteousness of the loving heavenly Father.

May they truly be "children of a greater God."

Great Reading for the Family

*Books for Reading Aloud
and Books for Young Readers*

AGE GROUPINGS:
    PS = preschoolers
    GS = ages 6-10
    YA = young adult
    AA = all ages

Note: All these categories are imprecise and will depend upon the maturity and attention span of your children. They serve only as the roughest guide to the level of difficulty in comprehending the book. Some children may not be yet ready to read these books but will enjoy having the story read aloud to them.

Aesop, *Fables*
    This Greek classic is a collection of short tales and proverbs which illustrate character strengths and flaws.

It is a rich treasure of moral teaching for both young and old. Make sure you get a modern translation as some of the older ones will, by their difficult language, obscure the messages in the stories. [AA]

Louisa May Alcott, *Little Women*
This book was my wife's favorite book as a child, and my two daughters have followed in her footsteps in appreciating its warm depiction of family life and its unflagging commitment to moral virtue. This book provides realistic, yet powerful examples of morality for children and adults alike. [GS/YA]

Hans Christian Andersen, *Fairy Tales*
Brothers Grimm, *Fairy Tales*
These two classic collections of fairy tales include most of the popular favorites. Be aware that the original versions are more violent and less prone to "happy endings" than some of the modern rewrites of these tales. These stories make good fodder for family discussions of moral values and how to deal with difficult situations. [PS/GS]

J. M. Barrie, *Peter Pan*
Charming adventure tale about a young boy who doesn't want to grow up. [GS/YA]

L. Frank Baum, *The Wizard of Oz*
Dorothy's adventures in Oz make for delightful and imagination-stirring reading. This story provides us with a powerful picture of our human search to overcome our inadequacies, along with the hope that the resources for change are always within our grasp. [GS/YA]

Michael Bedard, *Emily*
Who is this unusual reclusive neighbor who writes poetry? This is the story of a girl who discovers that her neighbor is the famous poet Emily Dickinson. [GS]

Ludwig Bemelmans, *Madeline*
This is the rhymed story of Madeline, the little girl who

is brave even in the face of having her appendix removed. [GS]

William J. Bennett, *The Book of Virtues*
An indispensible collection of stories and extracts grouped together by the character qualities they teach. You will find hours' worth of valuable material for the whole family contained between the covers of this hefty volume. [AA]

Christina Bjork, *Linnea in Monet's Garden*
A young girl visits the garden of the great painter Monet. This charming story affirms the importance of great art. [AA]

Michael Bond, *A Bear Called Paddington*
The humorous misadventures of a lovable, but none too bright bear, known for his oversized hat, yellow raincoat, and red Wellington boots. [AA]

Jan Brett, *Beauty and the Beast*
A version of the classic tale which teaches that beauty is more than skin deep and that true love involves sacrifice. [GS/YA]

Charlotte Bronte, *Jane Eyre*
Jane is an example of moral character in this mysterious and moving book. [YA]

Margaret Wise Brown, *Goodnight Moon*
A simple and soothing book to read to very young children before they go to bed. Its gentle rhythms seem to create an environment of peacefulness. [PS]

Jean de Brunhoff, *The Story of Babar*
A talking elephant's adventures in France and as king of the elephants. Delightful illustrations. [GS]

John Bunyan, *The Pilgrim's Progress*
> Classic Christian allegory of the spiritual life. The adaptation called *Dangerous Journey* (published by Eerdmans) puts the story within the reach of children without sacrificing its substance and power. [GS/YA]

Frances Hodgson Burnett, *The Secret Garden; The Little Princess*
> *The Secret Garden* is a magical tale about the transformation of an angry and selfish little girl through the healing power of love and friendship. *The Little Princess* teaches the virtues of compassion and consideration for others, even in the face of hardship. [YA]

Sheila Burnford, *The Incredible Journey*
> Exciting tale about two dogs and a cat who brave the wilds in search of their owner. [YA]

Lewis Carroll, *Alice's Adventures in Wonderland; Alice Through the Looking Glass*
> The Alice stories are marked by a seemingly endless supply of wit and invention. They can be thoroughly enjoyed by all ages, but most children will enjoy them more when they are a bit older. [AA]

Susan Coolidge, *What Katy Did*
> This story follows the development of character and virtue in a young girl after a crippling accident. [GS/YA]

Barbara Cooney, *Miss Rumphius*
> Miss Rumphius wishes to leave her mark on the world and finds a beautiful way to do it. [GS]

Roald Dahl, *Charlie and the Chocolate Factory*
> The humorous tale of a young boy whose goodness and decency earns him his dream. His fate is contrasted with those who are greedy, gluttonous, self-absorbed, and disobedient. [GS/YA]

Daniel Defoe, *Robinson Crusoe*
> Fascinating tale of a man stranded on a desert island who learns to survive with his meager store of food and tools. Defoe's tale has explicit references to the sovereignty of God and our need to trust in Him. The story raises many moral issues. [YA]

Tomie dePaola, *The Clown of God*
> The moving story of a beggar boy who becomes a famous juggler and learns to dedicate his gift to God. [AA]

Charles Dickens, *A Christmas Carol*
> Classic tale about a cruel and selfish man who discovers what is really important in life. [YA]

Arthur Conan Doyle, *Sherlock Holmes* stories
> Beginning with *A Study in Scarlet*, Doyle wrote four novels and numerous short stories about his fictional detective. Holmes is a model of how to use logical deductive thinking to solve problems. Children will love to curl up with one of these stories and lose themselves in the foggy streets of Edwardian London. They are exciting as well as intellectually challenging. The vocabulary is sometimes difficult, so they are recommended for older children. [YA]

Clifton Fadiman, *World Treasury of Children's Literature* (2 volumes)
> In these two volumes you will find some of the finest children's writing of all time: poetry, short stories, myths, and selections of longer stories. Both classic and modern pieces are included in this cornucopia of great children's literature. [AA]

Anne Frank, *The Diary of Anne Frank*
> The emotionally wrenching diary of a young girl whose family and friends suffer at the hands of Nazi Germany. Teaches valuable lessons about tolerance, loyalty, and the value of human life. [YA]

Don Freeman, *Corduroy*
An adorable bear finds the home he has always dreamed of. [PS/GS]

Kenneth Grahame, *The Wind in the Willows; The Reluctant Dragon*
The Wind in the Willows is a charming book with lovable characters and a deep sense of nostalgia for the innocence and wonder of childhood. Children enjoy its marvelous humor. *The Reluctant Dragon* is a delightful story of a precocious boy and his friendship with a lazy and cowardly dragon. Provides a model of how to explore difficult situations and find a positive solution. Its wry humor makes it a treat for adults as well. [AA]

Florence Parry Heide, *The Shrinking of Treehorn; Treehorn's Treasure*
Sophisticated and wryly humorous tales about a boy who is always ignored and the bizarre and unexpected things which happen to him. [GS/AA]

James Herriot, *All Creatures Great and Small*
The first in a series of books about a young English veterinarian in the Yorkshire countryside. [YA]

Russell Hoban, *Bedtime for Frances; A Baby Sister for Frances; Bread and Jam for Frances*
Children seem to find in Frances, a small and rather precocious badger, a mirror of their own fears, distastes, and faults. Positive picture of family life. *Bread and Jam for Frances* is a good tale for picky eaters. [GS]

Angela Elwell Hunt, *The Tale of Three Trees*
A rich allegorical folktale about what God has done for us. Three trees each have a dream. One tree wants to become a treasure chest, one a ship, and the third a sign for all mankind. Each of these dreams is fulfilled in unexpected ways by the power of God. [AA]

Hannah Hurnard, *Hind's Feet on High Places*
Allegorical tale about the Christian life, seen through the eyes of Much-Afraid as she goes in search of God's "high places." [YA]

Rudyard Kipling, *The Jungle Books*; *Just So Stories*
Much loved animal tales that teach us about humans and the way they treat each other. Many moral lessons and much humorous entertainment await the reader of Kipling's stories. [GS/YA]

Charles and Mary Lamb, *Tales from Shakespeare*
The Lambs manage to capture much of the power and beauty of Shakespeare's dramas in their prose renditions. While no substitute for the bard himself, these tales are a great introduction to the riches your children will find later in reading the original plays for themselves. [GS/YA]

Andrew Lang, *The Blue Fairy Book; The Red Fairy Book*
Two representatives in Lang's series of fairy tale collections. Each book is named after a color. These are unexpurgated originals, so be forewarned that the stories do not always have happy endings and are often a bit grisly. [GS/YA]

Munro Leaf, *The Story of Ferdinand*
Gentle Ferdinand is a peaceful bull who would rather sit and smell the flowers than fight in the ring. A touching story. [GS]

Madelyn L'Engle, *A Wrinkle in Time*
An exciting fantasy novel with underlying Christian themes. [YA]

C. S Lewis, *The Chronicles of Narnia* [*The Lion, the Witch and the Wardrobe; Prince Caspian; The Voyage of the Dawn Treader; The Silver Chair; The Magician's Nephew; The Horse and His Boy; The Last Battle*]

A series of books about four children who find their way into the land of Narnia where they experience exciting adventures which teach the reader about redemption, salvation, and the life of faith. Powerful theological insights are artfully cloaked in delightful allegorical tales. Older children and adults will also gain much pleasure and insight from Lewis' space trilogy and other of his many great books. [AA]

C. S. Lewis, *Letters to Children*
Readers who enjoyed the Chronicles of Narnia will be interested in these letters, many of which discuss the meaning and origin of the Narnian tales. [YA]

Arnold Lobel, *Frog and Toad Are Friends*
A collection of simple stories demonstrating the power of true friendship. [PS/GS]

Hugh Lofting, *Doctor Doolittle*
Humorous adventures of a man who "talked with the animals." [GS/YA]

Jack London, *The Call of the Wild*
Thrilling page-turner that chronicles the life of an arctic sled dog. Its intensity makes it more suitable for older children. [YA]

Leanne Lucas, *Addie McCormick* stories
Series of mystery novels for young girls in the Nancy Drew mold, but with an explicit Christian message. My nine-year-old loves them. [YA]

George MacDonald, *The Golden Key; The Princess and the Goblin; The Princess and Curdie; At the Back of the North Wind*
These fantasy-adventure stories communicate powerful images of the spiritual life and the path to spiritual maturity. *At the Back of the North Wind* is helpful for children who are dealing with death. MacDonald is a writer of peculiar depth and insight. [AA]

George MacDonald, *Sir Gibbie*
This novel for adults will also be enjoyed by children for its portrayal of a young orphan who learns about his magnificent and unexpected identity. [YA/AA]

Catherine Marshall, *Christy*
This is a novel based upon the true experiences of a young woman sent to teach in the Appalachian mountains in 1912. [YA]

Robert McCloskey, *Make Way for Ducklings*
A family of ducks face the perils of city life. [GS]

Henrietta C. Mears, *What the Bible is All About for Young Explorers*
This resource will help children better understand the Bible. Contains overviews of each book of the Bible, themes, outlines, and important background information. [GS/YA]

A. A. Milne, *When We Were Very Young; Now We Are Six*
Every child should grow up familiar with these marvelous rhymes and poems. They are charming, disarming, and funny. [PS/GS]

Winnie the Pooh; *The House at Pooh Corner*
The warm and humorous adventures of Winnie the Pooh and his friends. [AA]

Lucy Montgomery, *Anne of Green Gables*
Instead of the orphan boy they had hoped for, a spinster and her brother are sent young Anne by mistake. Anne's precocious imagination gets her into (and out of) a number of adventures. [YA]

Mary Norton, *The Borrowers*
The adventures of tiny people who secretly live in, and borrow from, the homes of the regular-sized. Fun adventures for kids. [YA]

Charles Perrault, *Fairy Tales; Mother Goose Rhymes*
Undisputed classics that all children will be sure to love.
[PS/GS]

Watty Piper, *The Little Engine That Could*
Charming tale which teaches us that perseverance and
hard work will pay off, as will a positive attitude to the
struggles we face in life. [PS/GS]

Chaim Potok, *The Chosen*
Both young and old readers will gain much from this
powerful novel about the physical, spiritual, and intellectual coming of age of two young Jewish boys. Full of rich
insights, it makes a valuable statement about toleration.
[YA]

Beatrix Potter, *Peter Rabbit and Other Tales*
Peter is an overly curious rabbit who disobeys his mother
and almost gets caught by Mr. McGregor. Lovely illustrations highlight these simple tales. [PS/GS]

Howard Pyle, *The Adventures of Robin Hood*
Exciting adventures of the man who "stole from the rich
to give to the poor." [YA]

H. A. Rey, *Curious George; Curious George Rides a Bike;
Curious George Flies a Kite*
George is a monkey who cannot keep himself out of
trouble. Unfailingly, he is always rescued by his friend,
the Man With the Yellow Hat. [PS/GS]

Barbara Robinson, *The Best Christmas Pageant Ever*
The story of how the mean and unruly Herdman kids
taught the rest of the church the true meaning of
Christmas. Fall-down funny with a powerful message.
[AA]

William F. Russell, *Classic Myths to Read Aloud*
The classic Greek and Roman myths are a gold mine of

moral instruction. Russell has written them at a level suitable for young children and has retained their mystery and dignity. Great discussion-starters on moral issues. [GS/YA]

William F. Russell, *Classics to Read Aloud to Your Children; More Classics to Read Aloud to Your Children*
Valuable collection of excerpts from the classics which will whet the appetite of your children for great books. Age-graded, with helpful introductions and vocabulary guides. [AA]

Maurice Sendak, *Where the Wild Things Are*
Some parents have used this book about friendly monsters as an antidote to the fear of nightmares. *There's a Nightmare in My Closet* by Mercer Mayer is equally good for this problem area. [GS]

Doctor Seuss, *The Cat in the Hat; Horton Hears a Who*
The stories of Dr. Seuss are a good introduction to the pleasures of language, filled with nonsense and creativity. Many, like *Horton Hears a Who*, teach important lessons. The message "a person's a person, no matter how small" has special poignancy in this day of rampant abortions. [PS/GS]

Anna Sewell, *Black Beauty*
A good story and a passionate critique of cruelty to animals. [YA]

Margery Sharp, *The Rescuers*
Exciting story of the brave mice of the Prisoner's Aid Society, who help mice all over the world out of various troubles. [GS/YA]

Isaac Bashevis Singer, *Children's Stories*
Humorous and poignant stories by a gifted Yiddish storyteller. "Zlateh the Goat" is especially moving. [AA]

Esphyr Slobodkina, *Caps for Sale*
The adventures of a cap peddler whose caps are stolen by mischievous monkeys. [GS]

Patricia St. John, *Treasures in the Snow*
When her little brother is crippled by the town bully, Annette sets out to gain revenge and learns about anger, hatred, and forgiveness. This and other St. John books are distinguished by their powerful Christian messages. [YA]

William Steig, *Yellow and Pink*
A funny little parable that makes a powerful argument that humans are not the result of chaos or mindless evolution, but the creation of God. Subtle and profound. [GS/AA]

Robert Louis Stevenson, *A Child's Garden of Verses*
Simple little poems that children of many generations have treasured. [PS/GS]

Robert Louis Stevenson, *Treasure Island*
Classic pirate tale sure to delight most young shipmates! [YA]

Adrien Stoutenburg, *American Tall Tales*
The stories of Paul Bunyan, Pecos Bill, Davy Crockett, Johnny Appleseed, and others stretch our imaginations and our credulity. [GS/YA]

Rosemary Sutcliff, *The Sword and the Circle*
Brilliant retellings of Arthurian Britain and the knights of the round table. [YA]

Jonathan Swift, *Gulliver's Travels*
Brilliant and humorous insights on human nature through the eyes of the intrepid traveler, Gulliver. Parts of this book are suitable for children; other sections are best left for young adults. [YA]

Corrie Ten Boom, *The Hiding Place*

Heroic true story of Corrie Ten Boom and her sister, who endure the hardships of a Nazi concentration camp by the strength of their faith and trust in God. Though intense in its depiction of evil, the triumph of righteousness makes this worthwhile reading for adults and children alike. [YA]

J. R. R. Tolkien, *The Hobbit; The Lord of the Rings [The Fellowship of the Ring; The Two Towers; The Return of the King]; Farmer Giles of Ham*

Tolkien's stories celebrate heroism and appreciation for the simple things in life. They are tales of the battle between good and evil that will excite the reader and challenge his imagination. Tolkien's Christian worldview comes through in subtle and powerful ways. *The Hobbit* and *Farmer Giles* are appropriate for younger children, but *The Lord of the Rings* is more sophisticated and demanding. [YA]

Mark Twain, *The Adventures of Tom Sawyer; The Adventures of Huckleberry Finn*

You'll laugh and thrill to the adventures of two intrepid explorers, Tom and Huck. May need to be edited for younger listeners, but this is a book the entire family will be sure to enjoy. [YA/AA]

Judith Viorst, *Alexander and the Terrible, Horrible, No Good, Very Bad Day*

Alexander has one of those days when everything seems to go wrong, and we find ourselves feeling both empathy and humor. The kind of book to turn a bad day around and bring a smile to the face of even the most grumpy. [GS/AA]

Walter Wangerin, *The Book of the Dun Cow; Potter*

Wangerin is a contemporary Christian writer of abundant insight and writing talent. His vocabulary is difficult at times, but your children will find him worth the effort. [YA]

Rosemary Wells, *Morris's Disappearing Bag*
One of the many slyly amusing stories by Rosemary Wells. In this one, Morris gets back at his big sisters and brother who tell him he is too little to play with their toys. [GS]

E.B. White, *Charlotte's Web*
This wise and eloquent story about the friendship between a pig and a spider is one of the most popular of modern children's stories. White's prose is a model of good writing. [GS/AA]

Laura Ingalls Wilder, *Little House on the Prairie* series
The nine books of the Little House series are based on Laura's prairie childhood. They reflect a family lifestyle based on Christian values, hard work, and mutual love and respect. Your children will see moral virtue in action in this unforgettable set of books. Great for reading aloud. [AA]

Margery Williams, *Velveteen Rabbit*
Beautiful story about a stuffed animal who becomes real through the love of his young owner. [GS/AA]

Gene Zion, *Harry the Dirty Dog*
A great story for kids who balk at taking a bath. [GS]

Notes

Chapter 1—Being Moral in a Time of Relativism

1. Ron Julian, *McKenzie Study Center News and Views*, Nov. 1993.
2. Ronald Allen, *Imagination* (Portland, OR: Multnomah Press).

Chapter 2—Going Beyond the Rules

1. William J. Bennett, *The De-Valuing of America* (New York: Simon and Schuster, 1992), p. 166.
2. C. S. Lewis, *Mere Christianity* (New York: Macmillan, 1952), p. 77.
3. G. K. Chesterton, *Tremendous Trifles* (New York: Dodd, Mead and Co., 1917), p. 14.
4. Seneca, *Letters to Lucius*, 90.
5. Ibid., *Quaestiones Naturales*, III, 30.
6. C. S. Lewis, *The Abolition of Man* (New York: Macmillan, 1947), p. 88.
7. Augustine, *The City of God*, V, 19.

Chapter 3—What Does Virtue Look Like?

1. James Q. Wilson, *The Moral Sense* (New York: Free Press, 1993).
2. Peter Kreeft, *Fundamentals of the Faith* (San Francisco: Ignatius Press, 1988), p. 176.

Chapter 4—Making a Habit of Virtue

1. Charlotte Mason, *Home Education* (Wheaton, IL: Tyndale House, 1989), p. 106.

Chapter 5—Thinking Christianly

1. C. S. Lewis, *The Weight of Glory* (New York: Macmillan, 1949), pp. 28-29.
2. Steve Turner, *Up to Date* (Belleville, MI: Lion, 1985), pp. 138-39.

Chapter 6—Every Child a Theologian

1. Dorothy L. Sayers, *The Whimsical Christian* (New York: Macmillan, 1978), p. 26.
2. Soren Kierkegaard, *The Journals of Kierkegaard* (London: Fontana Books, 1958), p. 53.
3. G. K. Chesterton, *The New Jerusalem* (London: Hodder and Stoughton, 1920), p. 110.
4. Frederick Buechner, *Wishful Thinking* (New York: Harper and Row, 1973), p. 91.
5. In Michael Bauman, *Roundtable: Conversations with European Theologians* (Grand Rapids: Baker, 1990), p. 102.
6. Charles Dickens, *Hard Times* (New York: Bantam Books, 1964), p. 4.
7. Helmut Thielicke, *A Little Exercise for Young Theologians* (Grand Rapids: Eerdmans, 1962), p. 17.
8. C. S. Lewis, *God in the Dock* (Grand Rapids: Eerdmans, 1970), p. 98.

Chapter 7—In Praise of Tradition

1. G. K. Chesterton, *Orthodoxy* (New York: Dodd, Mead and Co., 1955), p. 85.
2. T. S. Eliot, *The Selected Prose of T. S. Eliot* (New York: Harcourt, Brace, Jovanovich, 1975), p. 38.
3. Ibid., *The Sacred Wood* (London: Methuen, 1928), p. 52.
4. C. S. Lewis, *Surprised by Joy* (New York: Harcourt, Brace, Jovanovich, 1955), pp. 207-08.
5. In Os Guiness and John Seel, *No God But God* (Chicago: Moody, 1992), p. 199.
6. T-Bone Burnett, liner notes to Maria Muldaur album "Gospel Nights," Takoma Records, 1980.

Chapter 8—Spoiling the Egyptians

1. Augustine, *On Christian Doctrine*, II, xl.

236

2. John Calvin, *Institutes of the Christian Religion*, II, ii, xv.
3. Francis A. Schaeffer, "Two Contents, Two Realities," in *The Complete Works of Francis A. Schaeffer*, vol. 3 (Westchester, IL: Crossway Books, 1982), p. 412.

Chapter 9—The Spiritual Lives of Children

1. Walter Wangerin, *The Orphean Passages* (New York: Harper and Row, 1986), pp. 20-22.

Chapter 10—The Moral Imagination and Culture

1. Harry S. Broudy, *Enlightened Cherishing* (Bloomington: Indiana University Press, 1994), p. 37.

Chapter 11—Television: The One-Eyed Bandit

1. Bill McKibben, *The Age of Missing Information* (New York: Plume, 1993), pp. 22-23.

Chapter 12—The Adventure of Reading Aloud

1. C. S Lewis, *Surprised by Joy* (New York: Harcourt, Brace, Jovanovich, 1955), p. 10.

Chapter 13—The Moral Value of Stories

1. William Kirk Kilpatrick, *Psychological Seduction* (Nashville: Thomas Nelson, 1983), pp. 119-20.
2. Alistair MacIntyre, *After Virtue* (Notre Dame, IN: University of Notre Dame Press, 1984), p. 216.

Chapter 14—The True and the Beautiful

1. Dorothy L. Sayers, *The Mind of the Maker* (New York: Harper and Row, 1941), p. 22.
2. George MacDonald, *Sir Gibbie* (London: J. M. Dent and Sons, 1911), p. 437.
3. Annie Dillard, *A Pilgrim at Tinker Creek* (New York: Harper and Row, 1974), pp. 15-16.
4. Leland Ryken, *The Liberated Imagination* (Wheaton, IL: Harold Shaw Publishers, 1989), p. 28.

Chapter 15—Music to Calm the Savage Breast

1. Arnold Schopenhauer, *The World as Will and Idea*, vol. 1, p. 52.
2. Plato, *The Republic*, III, 401B.
3. Peter Kreeft, *Making Choices* (Ann Arbor, MI: Servant, 1990), p. 134.

Chapter 17—The Road to Christian Adulthood

1. Charles Spurgeon, *Christ's Incarnation* (Pasadena, TX: Pilgrim Publications, 1978), p. 98.

Other Good Harvest House Reading

HOW TO STUDY THE BIBLE FOR YOURSELF
by *Tim LaHaye*

This excellent book provides fascinating study helps and charts that will make personal Bible study more interesting and exciting. A three-year program is outlined for a good working knowledge of the Bible.

THE INTERNATIONAL INDUCTIVE STUDY BIBLE

This first of its kind in Bible publishing history, *The International Inductive Study Bible* teaches you how to unearth the treasures of God's Word for yourself using a simple, proven step-by-step plan. Includes four-color maps and charts, a concordance, and unique study helps.

LOVING GOD WITH ALL YOUR MIND
by *Elizabeth George*

In a fresh, friendly manner, Elizabeth George explores what it means to think biblically. "Biblical thinking," she writes, "gives women freedom from the draining emotions of fear, worry, depression, and bitterness." Liz will help you develop a scriptural and healthy view of God, the past, the future, problems, other people, and yourself, based on six truths backed by God's promises and power.

DADDY, I BLEW UP THE SHED!
by *Phil Callaway*

Through his ordinary adventures as an everyday guy, Phil shares his wit and wisdom on topics as varied as the crazy things kids do, the tender moments between mother and son, and why Dad knows everything. In this lighthearted and inspiring look at family life, you'll recognize your spouse, your kids, your parents—even yourself!

TRAIN UP A CHILD

Train Up a Child is filled with 356 quick devotions that even the most active youngsters will listen to. Each devotion is simple, creative, and interactive. Make learning about God a fun part of every day, while sowing seeds of faith that will grow as your child does!

Dear Reader:

We would appreciate hearing from you regarding this Harvest House nonfiction book. It will enable us to continue to give you the best in Christian publishing.

1. What most influenced you to purchase *Children of a Greater God*?
   ☐ Author   ☐ Recommendations
   ☐ Subject matter   ☐ Cover/Title
   ☐ Backcover copy   ☐ _____

2. Where did you purchase this book?
   ☐ Christian bookstore   ☐ Grocery store
   ☐ General bookstore   ☐ Other
   ☐ Department store

3. Your overall rating of this book:
   ☐ Excellent   ☐ Very good   ☐ Good   ☐ Fair   ☐ Poor

4. How likely would you be to purchase other books by this author?
   ☐ Very likely   ☐ Not very likely
   ☐ Somewhat likely   ☐ Not at all

5. What types of books most interest you? (check all that apply)
   ☐ Women's Books   ☐ Fiction
   ☐ Marriage Books   ☐ Biographies
   ☐ Current Issues   ☐ Children's Books
   ☐ Christian Living   ☐ Youth Books
   ☐ Bible Studies   ☐ Other _____

6. Please check the box next to your age group.
   ☐ Under 18   ☐ 25-34   ☐ 45-54
   ☐ 18-24   ☐ 35-44   ☐ 55 and over

Mail to: Editorial Director
Harvest House Publishers
1075 Arrowsmith
Eugene, OR 97402

Name _____

Address _____

City _____ State _____ Zip _____

**Thank you for helping us to help you
in future publications!**